ISBN 978-1-332-76780-9
PIBN 10439527

This book is a reproduction of an important historical work. Forgotten Books uses
state-of-the-art technology to digitally reconstruct the work, preserving the original format
whilst repairing imperfections present in the aged copy. In rare cases, an imperfection in
the original, such as a blemish or missing page, may be replicated in our edition. We do,
however, repair the vast majority of imperfections successfully; any imperfections that
remain are intentionally left to preserve the state of such historical works.

1 MONTH OF
FREE
READING

at

www.ForgottenBooks.com

By purchasing this book you are eligible for one month membership to ForgottenBooks.com, giving you unlimited access to our entire collection of over 700,000 titles via our web site and mobile apps.

To claim your free month visit:
www.forgottenbooks.com/free439527

English
Français
Deutsche
Italiano
Español
Português

www.forgottenbooks.com

Mythology Photography **Fiction**
Fishing Christianity **Art** Cooking
Essays Buddhism Freemasonry
Medicine **Biology** Music **Ancient
Egypt** Evolution Carpentry Physics
Dance Geology **Mathematics** Fitness
Shakespeare **Folklore** Yoga Marketing
Confidence Immortality Biographies
Poetry **Psychology** Witchcraft
Electronics Chemistry History **Law**
Accounting **Philosophy** Anthropology
Alchemy Drama Quantum Mechanics
Atheism Sexual Health **Ancient History**
Entrepreneurship Languages Sport
Paleontology Needlework Islam
Metaphysics Investment Archaeology
Parenting Statistics Criminology
Motivational

WITNESSES
to the
HORROR

Cecile Holmes White

To/
Dr. J. F. Skinner

With a fervent hope that
a book like this will never
have to be written again

[signature]

WITNESSES TO THE HORROR

North Carolinians Remember the Holocaust

By
Cecile Holmes White

Published in cooperation with
NORTH CAROLINA COUNCIL ON THE HOLOCAUST

Witnesses to the Horror

Copyright ©1987 Cecile Holmes White

Printed in the United States of America

DEDICATION

This book is dedicated to the millions of Jews and Christians who did not survive the Holocaust, and to the Allied servicemen who died trying to liberate them from Adolf Hitler's Third Reich.

PREFACE

Writing this book has taught me that a strong support network is the most important element in being able to complete any task. While I have hundreds of hours invested in this, my own time comprises only a fraction of the effort put forth by so many other people.

For their unfailing support, patience and encouragement, I first want to thank Rabbi Arnold S. Task and Mr. Morris Kiel. Thanks must go also to the North Carolina Council on the Holocaust for supporting this project. And I owe a great debt to each survivor and liberator who was interviewed for this book. Moreover, this book would not have been possible without financial support from the Sigmund Sternberger Foundation and the Z. Smith Reynolds Foundation.

In the several years I have worked on this project, colleagues, friends and relatives — especially my husband, Kenny, have listened to me and kept me from giving up when I was most frustrated or suffering an acute case of writer's block. Many of them, including my parents, Anne S. and James G. Holmes, read parts of the manuscripts and offered insightful suggestions.

For reading the entire manuscript and helping me shape it into a book, my thanks go especially to Dr. Sidney Bolkosky of the University of Michigan-Dearborn, Cole C. Campbell of the *Greensboro News & Record* and Dr. Karl A. Schleunes of the University of North Carolina at Greensboro.

Through reference books, follow-up interviews and other forms of research, every effort has been made to ensure that the events and experiences described here are accurate. In quoted sections, the testimony of each survivor or liberator has, in most instances, been included exactly as it was said. (A professional firm specializing in court depositions transcribed each taped interview.) Individual testimonies, if edited, were edited only if the survivor or liberator requested such a change or if a particular remark or description, as said, would have been unclear to the reader.

Cecile Holmes White
September 1987

TABLE OF CONTENTS

INTRODUCTION

After winning the war, Adolf Hitler intended to establish what he called a New European Order. Plans for that New Order had long been formulating in his brain, their outline firmly set in his racist conception of history. Nazi domination — military, political, economic — of conquered Europe he believed was justified by German racial superiority. The numerous Slavic peoples of eastern Europe, all of them "inferior," he planned to employ as slave laborers for their new German overlords.

Above all, however, Hitler wanted his New Order free of Jews. Jews were to him the source of all evil in the world. Their eradication would remove that source and prepare the way for superior Aryans to refashion a racially perfect world.

From the time of their founding as a political party in a Munich beer hall in 1919, the Nazis spoke of a "Jewish Problem." Anti-Semitism was the heart of their racist ideology and the central theme in their propaganda throughout the 1920s; a solution to the "Jewish Problem" as the basis for German rejuvenation was their most consistent promise.

The Nazi search for a solution to the Jewish problem began when they came to power in Berlin in 1933. Ultimately that search led to what the Nazis in their bureaucratic terminology called the "Final Solution to the Jewish Problem." Six million Jews are thought to have died as a consequence of this Final Solution. Other "inferior" peoples were its victims as well. The Nazis killed a half million Gypsies and perhaps as many as five million Slavs. Upon the corpses of these people, deemed inferior and evil by the distorted Nazi vision, was to stand Hitler's New Order.

The people who tell their story in this book are witnesses to the horror wrought by the Nazis, witnesses to the most notorious disaster in the long sweep of human history. Either as victims of the disaster or as soldiers who helped bring it to an end, each one of them relates a direct experience with the Final Solution. Each one of them, either as inmate or liberator, has experience with a concentration or death camp in which the Nazis produced their Final Solution.

The names of these camps — Auschwitz, Treblinka, Sobibor, Chelmno, Majdanek, Belzec, to name only those the Nazis formally designated as extermination camps — have seared themselves into our consciousness. To speak their names is to utter a litany to the horrors of this century. They signify, writes English literary and social critic George Steiner, a second fall of man into sin, one as filled with unhappy implications about human beings and their nature as the story of man's first fall from Eden.

No designation of what happened in the Nazi camps, be it "Final Solution," "mass murder," or "the destruction of European Jewry," seems sufficient to capture the full import of its horror. The longing to embrace this horror in its fullness has led in recent years to the use of the term Holocaust, the hope being that it might convey meaning in a way other designations did not. Greek in origin, "Holocaust" means a complete sacrifice consumed by fire (a whole burnt offering), and for that reason does justice, its proponents argue, to the grisly work of the gas chambers and crematoria of Auschwitz and its sister camps.

There are those, however, who object to calling the Nazi crimes a Holocaust. The psychologist Bruno Bettelheim, himself a survivor of the Nazi camp at Buchenwald, rejects it because of the association it suggests between the most vicious of mass murders and ancient rituals of a profoundly religious nature. The association he finds sacrilegious, profaning to both God and man.

Far more important than whether the disaster is called a Holocaust or a Final Solution is the recognition that it was manmade; that its origins lie not in the reaches of a remote outer darkness — but in the depths of an inner one.

Equally crucial are the questions that this disaster raises. What propels one group of men to erect factories in which they produce the deaths of other men? Are the circumstances in which such things necessarily occur extraordinary ones, or could they possibly be ordinary? Is the evil at work here incomprehensible, larger than life, or is it, as Hannah Arendt suggests, banal, the work of ordinary little men? Why was it the Jews upon whom the Nazis focused their racism? What went wrong with the nineteenth-century assimilation of Jews into German society, a process once regarded as the model of assimilation into a European culture?

How far back into history do we have to go to find answers to the questions raised by the Holocaust? Do we have to explore the entire range of the Jewish-Christian relationship, or can we concentrate our search upon modern Germany?

These questions intrude themselves into the lives of each of the persons interviewed in this book. Some will ask these questions directly; others obliquely. As readers we cannot avoid asking them either; neither can we avoid looking for answers.

Coherent answers to these questions are likely to be found somewhere within the framework that the questions themselves suggest — a framework that consists, on the one side of a consideration of Jewish-Christian relations — and, on the others, by the growth of 19th-century racism, by the emergence of the so-called modern Jewish Problem, by the effects of the sacrifices demanded of Germans during World War I, by the circumstances in the 1920s that led to the growth of a National Socialist German Workers' Party (the Nazis), and, finally, by the way in which Nazi Jewish policy was made after 1933.

******

Adolf Hitler and the Nazis rejected nearly every basic tenet of Christianity, a fact that at first glance raises doubt that examination of the long relationship between Jews and Christians can be useful for answering any of the questions raised by the Holocaust. To be sure, tensions between Jews and Christians stretch back to the first centuries of what came to be called the Christian era, to the time when adherents of both religions sought and found (with roughly equal success, apparently) converts among the peoples of the far-flung Roman Empire. A modern Christian theologian likens the tensions between Judaism and Christianity during these centuries to that of a sibling rivalry. Not until the fourth century, when the Emperor Theodosias decreed Christianity to be the official Roman religion, did the younger of these siblings emerge as dominant.

The most dangerous legacy of that rivalry is the one that branded Jews as responsible for the crucifixion of Jesus, the man Christians believed to be both the son of God and the messiah. Technically, of course, the Romans crucified Jesus, but his earliest biographers sought to place at least part of the onus upon the Jews. Although he was a Jew himself, the Jews had rejected Jesus as their messiah. Therein was the basis for tensions and resentments. Describing the crucifixion, the gospel-writer Matthew recounts the story of the Jewish crowd that rejected the Roman governor's offer to free Jesus and called instead for the release of the notorious criminal Barabbas. The crowd, realizing what it had done, cries out that "His blood be on us and on our children."

Christian theologians, the pre-eminent Augustine of Hippo (354-430) among them, removed some of this onus from the Jews. Augustine argued that God, the creator of time and history, had some hidden purpose when he allowed Jews to reject Jesus. Their eventual acceptance of him, Augustine said, would herald the return of Christ to earth and introduce the millenium, or God's full perfection, into the affairs of this world.

Although Augustine's explanation became the official doctrine of the Church, it never took full root in the minds of uneducated Christians. During the centuries following Augustine, as Christianity became the foundation for an emerging European civilization, the image of Jews as the crucifiers of Christ remained a basic element of "folk Christianity."

The 19th and early 20th centuries found it no weaker than the 12th or 13th. This gruesome image remains a deep reservoir for anti-Jewish resentments that anti-Semites, Hitler included, have continuously drawn upon.

A second legacy of Christianity that has seriously complicated Jewish-Christian relations labels Jews as moneylenders and usurers. The stereotype of the usurious Jew extracting an exorbitant rate of interest from a Christian client, a staple in anti-Semitic lore, can be traced to the 11th and 12th centuries. Ironically, its origins lie in the efforts of Christians to clean up their own usurious activities. These attempts to purify the financial practices of the church and its agencies may appropriately be described as the first Christian reformation. The impulse to purification relates the reform efforts of St. Francis and St. Dominic, both of whom sought to re-emphasize the spiritual, non-materialist teachings of Christ. Christianity once again restated poverty as a Christian ideal; the taking of interest on a loan was condemned as against the laws of the church.

The Church's condemnation of usury coincided, in Western Europe at least, with an age of commercial expansion. Maintenance of that expansion depended very heavily upon moneylending, and moneylending upon the charge of interest. Christians continued to lend money and charge interest, presumably with a guilty conscience, although the church itself gradually withdrew from the practice. Jews, however, could engage in moneylending with impunity and Christians urged them to do so. Were not Jews condemned anyhow for their rejection of Christ? With Jews as moneylenders could not Christians continue to profit in commerce without damage either to their consciences or to their souls? So Christians justified themselves.

Competition presented by Jewish moneylenders created economic resentments in the commercial centers of Western Europe that during the next centuries contributed to the periodic expulsion of Jews. England, France, Spain, and various of the German states expelled their Jews from about 1300 to 1500. In economically backward Eastern Europe rulers hoped that moneylenders might yield greater commerce; therefore the effect of these expulsions was to move large numbers of Jews into Poland and western Russia.

A medieval Europe that explained its economic system, its social structure, and its political organization in Christian terms inevitably defined the Jew as an outsider, a status that left the small Jewish minority extremely vulnerable. As a people, as a culture, as a religion, Jews and Judaism were regarded by Christian Europeans as inferior. As best they were seen as religious and cultural museum pieces in a world that had far surpassed them. Only by converting to Christianity could Jews enter the mainstream of European culture. Despite persecutions — or because of them, perhaps — a few Jews chose to take that step.

Prospects for dramatic change in Jewish-Christian relations did not present themselves until the Enlightenment of the 18th century. Rejecting much of the Christian tradition, thinkers of the Enlightenment talked about reorganizing, and thereby improving, the world along lines dictated by their own reason. Reason seemed to dictate that the differences between people were more apparent than real; the implications for relations between

Christians and Jews were profound. Jews might well be adhering to an outmoded religious superstition but only because of insufficient enlightenment, not because of an innate inferiority. In 1781 an enlightened German official could write a pamphlet "On the Civic Improvement of the Jews" arguing that the Jewish character and inferior status were the product of Christian prejudice rather than inherent Jewish traits. The improvement of Jews depended upon their emancipation from both Judaism and from the prejudices of Christians, just as the emancipation of Christians depended upon the rejection of their own religious superstitions.

For European Jewry as a whole the French Revolution initiated legal emancipation from inferior status assigned during the Middle Ages. In France an emancipation decree in 1791 fulfilled the promise of the Enlightenment. For the first time a European society recognized Jews as full and equal citizens. In Germany the first emancipation decree came in Bavaria in 1809; Prussia's came in 1812; most other states quickly followed suit. Elsewhere in Europe legal emancipation may have come more slowly, but it came nonetheless.

Legal emancipation was for Jews an invitation to become Europeans, be it as Frenchmen, Germans, Italians, or the like. The price implied was that they cease being Jews. They were to leave behind Judaism as a religion and a culture. In theory, at least the secularization of European culture was to ease their entry into the new world of post-revolutionary Europe.

Even in retrospect, the story of the assimilation of Jews into the 19th-century European worlds of politics, economics and culture seems one of remarkable success, and nowhere did this success appear more evident than in Germany. Enriched immeasureably by the contributions of Jews, German represented what one Jewish leader called "a safe harbor." Felix Mendelssohn in music, Heinrich Heine in poetry, Max Liebermann in painting and the thousands of other Jews who became physicians, scientists, academicians, lawyers, politicians and businessmen helped give German culture, education and industry the dynamism and prestige it enjoyed by the late 19th century. The distinctions between German and Jew, once so clear, seemed on the verge of ing that disappearance, fearing that the Jewish community itself might disappear in the process.

German Jews dramatically demonstrated their enthusiasm for German culture, the German nation and German society by means of their contribution to the German war effort in World War I: 80,000 Jews served in the German army; 35,000 were decorated for valor; 12,000 died for the Fatherland. Given a Jewish population of no more than 500,000 (about 1 percent of the German total), the contribution of Jews to the defense of German was proportionally higher than for non-Jews.

History paints a dark underside to this portrait of the assimilation of Jews into German society. Not everyone welcomed their adoption of German culture. Old resentments and stereotypes persisted; new ones were being created. Some Germans blamed Jews for the economic depression of the 1870s; others for the growth of the huge impersonal urban centers, for the onset of the industrial age, for the socialism that threatened to overthrow the world of Imperial Germany; still others for the modernism that rendered incomprehensible so much of the music, art and literature of the late 19th and early 20th centuries.

The development of racist ideologies during the second half of the 19th century served to embrace many of these new resentments as well as provide a new framework for many of the old ones. Racism was a European-wide phenomenon, no more serious in Germany, it seemed, than in other European countries. Racist explanations of history abounded in late 19th-century Germany, just as they did elsewhere.

German racists naturally posited the superior race to be of Germanic origin, although the concept of Germanic was usually thought to include the peoples of England, Holland, and Scandinavia. The best evidence for the superiority of the Germans — also called Nordics and Aryans — the racists discovered in the political, economic, military, and cultural power of England and Germany, the world's two greatest powers at the beginning of the 20th century. The general backwardness of Eastern Europe revealed to these racists the inferiority of other races.

Jews did not figure prominently in all racist ideologies, but in some they were designated the most inferior of all the races, a people thought to be without culture who could live only as parasites upon a larger host. In its most extreme form this racism held Jews to be the ultimate source of evil, the cause of all the problems besetting the modern, urban, industrial world.

World War I brought these racist ideologies from the outer edge to the center of life in Germany. From its beginnings, racism appealed largely to those on society's fringe, those least successful in the competition of the urban, industrial world. The insecurity and bitterness accumulating in these circles found easy explanation in a racism that could pinpoint the source of evil in the modern world as well as provide a pseudo-scientific basis for the desire to be superior.

Fueled by the rancor that collected in Germany as a result of World War I and its aftermath, racism grew during the 1920s into the monster of National Socialism. Nazi ideology was little more than a shopping list of resentments that began with the defeat in 1918 and ended with the depression of 1929. Defeat in the war, the war-guilt clause of the Treaty of Versailles, the horrendous inflation of 1923 — all worked to give Adolf Hitler and the Nazis an audience. Holding these together was anti-Semitism. Logical contradictions were papered over by a deep hatred of Jews, who were blamed for all of Germany's problems.

In January 1933 Hitler and the Nazis came to power already committed, emotionally and politically, to solving Germany's "Jewish Problem." For all the depth of that commitment, however, they had no clear notion of what form such a solution should take. They knew only that it should be drastic and complete

The result was that many Nazi agencies defined their own Jewish policies, often in contradiction and almost always in bitter competition with each other. Joseph Goebbels, Hitler's Propaganda Minister, hoped to gain control of the Jewish-owned press. Ernst Roehm planned to use his Stormtroopers to drive Jews out of their businesses and professions. These Stormtroopers arrested Jews by the thousands during the first months of Nazi rule, sometimes holding them for ransom and at other times throwing them into newly established concentration camps. Wilhelm Frick, Hitler's Minister of the Interior, produced legislative into German society. Heinrich Himmler's SS began looking into schemes that would facilitate the large-scale emigration of Jews from Germany. In a preliminary way, Hitler approved all of these efforts. His ultimate approval he would reserve for those efforts that gave the greatest promise of success.

The lack of a coordinating hand in Nazi Jewish policy did nothing to reduce the brutal effect upon its victims; in fact, the competition for control over Jewish policy may well have encouraged a brutality that a coordinated policy might temporarily, at least, have kept in closer check. Another example of this competition was a lack of logic or coherence in much of Nazi Jewish policy. It took until September 1935 for the Nazis to promulgate their infamous Nuremberg Laws which for the first time gave legal definition to the concept of the Jew and forbade marriage and sexual relations between Jew and Aryan. Given the Nazi belief that the inferiority of Jews lay in the impurity of their blood, logic alone would have suggested such a measure at the very beginning of Hitler's rule. Likewise, there was a contradiction between the Finance Ministry's financial restrictions that prevented Jews from taking their assets out of Germany and the efforts of the SS to promote the emigration of Jews.

Not until late 1938, after the "Night of Crystal" pogrom, did Hitler appoint his chief trouble shooter, Hermann Goering, to be the coordinator of Jewish policy. During the next two years there emerged under Goering's aegis the grandiose emigration schemes — the Lublin reservation and the Madagascar project — worked out mainly by the SS.

Any emigration schemes were rendered unworkable by the outbreak of war in September 1939. The war changed drastically the nature of the "Jewish Problem" by adding large numbers of Jews. The conquest of Poland brought nearly three million additional Jews under Nazi control, six times the number that had lived in Germany in 1933. Before Poland, the annexations of Austria and Czechoslovakia had already added a half million Jews. Another half million Jews lived in the territories conquered by the Nazis in 1940: Denmark, Norway, the Netherlands, Belgium, and France.

Nazi successes in Western Europe, however, paled in comparison to those in Eastern Europe following the June 1941 attack on Russia. Therewith the Nazi Jewish Problem was transformed completely. The roads to Moscow and Leningrad passed through the heartland of European Jewry, Russian-held Poland and Russia's own Pale of Settlement, which, with its eight to 10 million Jews contained the world's largest Jewish population. By December 1941 Adolf Hitler was at the height of his power. Nazi Germany controlled virtually the entire continent of Europe, from Paris in the west to the outskirts of Moscow in the east; from the outskirts of Leningrad in the north to Athens in the south. Hitler's New Order for Europe seemed within reach.

The centerpiece of that New Order, a Final Solution to the Jewish Problem, was already being constructed in 1941. SS execution squads followed the invading German army into Russia in June. By December these squads reported the shooting of one million Jews. Shooting proved to be a slow and cumbersome process. On December 8, 1941, the first experiments with the gassing of Jews took place in a concentration camp that the SS had established in Poland near Chelmno.

The Chelmno experiment proved successful in Nazi eyes. Gassing was a much more efficient way of killing people than shooting. As a result the SS established during the early months of 1942 five more death factories in eastern Europe, the largest and most important of which was named after the nearby town of Auschwitz. In these six camps, and in dozens of others, no less deadly for the lack of such designation, there was produced between late 1941 and early 1945 the Final Solution or what is now called the Holocaust.

In this book people who were witnesses to the horror of that Holocaust find their voices. To those voices we need to listen. They tell of unspeakable horror, of tragedy beyond comprehension, but they tell also of heroism and sacrifice that can redeem.

One of these voices belongs to Shelly Weiner, who as a child in Poland hid for three years from the Nazis. She tells of taking her own daughter to a gathering of Holocaust survivors in Washington, D.C. in April 1983 and seeing people who had suffered horrors of their own and gone on to lead meaningful and productive lives. These people, she tells her daughter, represent "a triumph for humanity ... They (The Nazis) didn't win in the end."

PROLOGUE

Like a chorus of irate workers blocked from their jobs by a potentially violent picket line, the witnesses queue up. Many are ready and willing to testify. They are the ones who suffered. Still others — the perpetrators and the bystanders — remain silent, unwilling to recount what they saw and what they did. But in the often jaded, sometimes overindulged ethos of 20th century America, few really want to listen to the witnesses who will talk. Even fewer are willing to listen long enough, thoroughly enough, and thoughtfully enough to understand the depth of the continuing revelation of human evil that unfolded as the Holocaust occurred.

It is a revelation of systematic genocide, a gradual unveiling of horror.

For most of us, it would be so much easier to consign the Holocaust to the musty confines of library shelves. We are far too uncomfortable when our living rooms are invaded by the faded black-and-white images of starved concentration camp internees with shaved heads and skeletal frames. Documentary or dramatization, any depiction of the Holocaust threatens to awaken our collective guilt. Even a generation removed from the events of World War II, the guilt affects us. If allowed to penetrate into the fertile soil of our consciousness, it all too easily could make us squirm, force us to remember that many Americans did too little, too late, to stop the obliteration of European Jewry.

Moreover, any comparison between this past and persecutions of the present (like the thousands of Jews being denied emigration by the Soviet Union) brings the Holocaust into even sharper focus. We may not be able to forget history, but, at least, the distance of time protects us. The clearer image of a present in which a propaganda machine of hate like that of Adolf Hitler in Nazi Germany might once again prevail across Europe, or some other continent, is hard for most of us to imagine. Even the detainment of the Soviet Jews, the virulent and violent anti-Semitism of American neo-Nazis, and the reassertion by fringe groups that the Holocaust never occurred do not awaken us.

It is easy to argue that that brick wall of disinterest is a natural one. After all, some say, what do the persecution and the slaughter of six million Jews and five million Christians, political protesters and others deemed unfit for life by the Nazis mean today? We forget that that slaughter was carried out by some citizens of the Third Reich, and allowed to happen by others. The slaughter was so systematic that thousands of pages of records and photographs were kept by the people doing the killing.

Still other skeptics ask: What does this horrible chapter of history mean in a largely affluent society thousands of miles from the Europe in which the Nazis almost succeeded in establishing a permanent totalitarian state?

Simplistic answers come easily. Adolf Hitler was a madman intent on world domination. His legacy must be studied. It must be studied by school children, professors, researchers and historians because of its significance.

But those are the easy answers.

They leave unexplained, unresolved and, most importantly, unexplored a much more devastating set of questions.

What does the Holocaust tell us about the good and evil dimensions of human nature? What does it tell us about the monstrous horror that festers under the twin sores of cultural and religious prejudice? What can we learn from the unrelenting faith of the witnesses who suffered, but who persistently believe that life has meaning in the wake and the aftermath of such suffering?

Jewish scholar Saul Friedlander[1] of Israel says that the Holocaust, like all of World War II, is an era that we can neither forget nor make our peace with. It is instead, he says, a time to which we keep returning, and an era we may always struggle to understand.

For years, the need to understand why it all happened was one of my last questions about the Holocaust. Like so many other white Southern Protestants, I grew up largely insulated from the first-hand experience of prejudice. Though I am a woman, I was neither the wrong race (black) nor the wrong religion (Jewish). The prejudice I did encounter was directed at other people, not at *me*.

When I first began intensive research through interviews with survivors of the Holocaust and the liberators of concentration camps in 1983, the work was part of my job as a full-time newspaper reporter. I was surprised to learn that there were survivors and liberators living less than five miles from my own home in Greensboro and in other cities across North Carolina. With candor and a polite hospitality that I soon recognized as typical of them, the survivors I interviewed invited me into their homes, made time to talk to me, and agreed to reiterate a past they have spend most of their lives trying to forget.

I finished my research, wrote, and saw published an article on survivors and liberators who live in the Triad area of North Carolina. The article appeared on April 10, 1983, that year the day of Yom Ha-Shoah, meaning "The Day of Destruction and Heroism." It is the day set aside in the Hebrew calendar as a day of remembrance for the victims of the Holocaust.

But completing the article left me restless, not contented. I couldn't forget the faces, the words, the everlasting "Why?" that crept into my every interview. I had become an unwitting participant in the effort to answer the darker, tougher questions posed by the revelation of evil. And I had begun to believe very deeply that others needed to know what the survivors, witnesses willing to talk about the evil, had told me. That is how this book came to be written.

Here are stories of living witnesses to the Holocaust. What they lived through and the moral implications of the Holocaust reek with the stink of human hatred. Peering into this well of torment is something all of us would rather avoid. The well reveals a dimension of life hard to look at, even harder to understand. We turn away. Yet the stories of these witnesses paint a portrait of human courage. It is a hopeful image.

Whether Jewish or non-Jewish, concentration camp survivor or liberator, these people experienced and remember what most of us find difficult to think about. These witnesses are the guardians of the revelation, the sentries at the sepulchre of the unknowable a tomb created by human hate, left sealed by human indifference.

May this volume help to break the seal.

CHAPTER 1
THREE SURVIVORS BEFORE THE WAR

Before World War II, the Jewish communities across Europe thrived. As early as medieval times, Jews in countries from Great Britain to Russia chose to live together in small clusters of homes gathered round a synagogue. Their reasons were multiple: physical safety in numbers, legal isolation making it easier to live with their own kind and the desire to preserve Jewish customs and traditions in predominantly Christian societies.[2]

By the 16th century, the ghettos in which Jews were forced to live were all over Europe. In eastern European nations, Jews sometimes lived in private towns called shtetls. The shtetl often was protected by the government, but its impact was the same as the ghetto: Jews were isolated, separated, and to a large degree, stigmatized as evil and different from the Christian world.

In eastern Europe, Jews in the ghetto often lived in abject poverty, nearly always hand-to-mouth. But they survived in those solid insular communities right up to the time of Hitler.

Life was different in western Europe. Freed after many of the ghettos were torn down at the end of the 18th century after Napoleon Bonaparte swept across the continent, many western

Burt Romer[3] was born into a Germany in which Jews were equal.

"I was born in Hennweiler, (now) West Germany," Romer says. "I was born in an intermarriage. My mother was Jewish, my father was Catholic. Since we had a Jewish mother, we automatically were considered Jewish. We were brought up in the Jewish faith completely."

The third son in the family, Berthold Romer (his German name) was only 6 years old when Adolf Hitler came to power.

"I went to school in 1932 — that year Hitler took power — and I was able to go to school until November 1938. That was when we had the Kristallnacht, what they call the Glass Night here.* After this happened, I was thrown out of school and I was branded and marked. I had to wear the Star of David on the outside of my clothing, whatever I wore — winter coat or sweater — and it specified Jew."

The simple change in apparel reflected a marked transition in his life and in the life of Jews across Germany. As the Third Reich rose, so declined the fortunes of Jews as Hitler re-awakened the sleeping anti-Semitism dormant in Germany since the close of World War I.

"Well, early, we had no problems with living. You were not marked, or branded. No one called you a Jew or anything like that because we were all from one country. But after Hitler took over, that's when it started."

The lines creasing Burt Romer's 59-year-old face deepen. He is thinking back, reaching behind the carefully-woven veil of memory that protects him from the past. It is not easy to recall feelings of the 6-year-old, the 10-year-old, the 12-year-old boy. It is not easy to think back to before the 18 months of hell he knew in Theresienstadt, a grisly labor camp about forty miles from Prague in Czechoslovakia where more than 33,000 Jews died.

Romer was 16 years old when he was arrested and taken to Theresienstadt. In the five years between Kristallnacht in 1938 and his arrest in May 1943, his life lost all sense of normality.

Wearing the Star of David was the first change. "It was not a

---

*NOTE: The day became known as 'Kristallnacht' because so many store windows were broken, so much glass was shattered.

pleasant feeling, because little children pointed their fingers at me or my brothers, called us Jews or spit at us," Romer says. "There was nowhere for us to go. You had to stay home, or if you went out, you'd better make sure that you had a tough piece of clothing on where you might be called a Jew. You had no more friends, you couldn't have any more friends. People were afraid. Especially you had to be careful that you were not talking to a girl, because this could cause you to be executed."

His part-Christian heritage kept Romer safe in the early years of the Third Reich. But it didn't protect his family from the Nazi police state.

In 1938, Romer's father lost his job. "My father lost his position with the government. He worked for the railroads, but it was a government position. He was in the navy, too ... until 1942. And then he was called to his commanding officer, and the commanding officer told him he could do anything he wanted to do if he would divorce my mother and leave the whole family. And he wouldn't do that, so he was discharged from the navy."

In 1942, the Nazis tightened the yoke. Romer's mother was taken on "6th of December 1942 to Auschwitz. And on the twelfth of December of '42' she was dead already. ... I would blame it quite a bit on certain individuals like Gestapo men in my home town, and two or three policeman who wanted us out of the way because we were the only ones left ... my father took it very hard. He went to Berlin — he saw Himmler, Bormann, all the ones in charge. They even promised him when he went to Berlin that my mother would come home in January, 1943 and she was dead already ... you remember her every year, the day she got killed. You go to the synagogue. I guess you never forget one of your family. It always will stay in your memory. It hurts, because you don't know what happened to her after she died. I presume she was cremated. What happened to her ashes, only God knows."

The fate of his two older brothers was similar. One died, the other survived four years in a concentration camp, but emerged a bitter, difficult man.

"And then, in 1942 ... I think (that's) when my oldest brother went to Buchenwald. His name was Roland, and he was 20 years old ... he worked in — in other words, they make lenses today. They worked for the government. He had to work, but he didn't

8

get full pay like anybody else ... and he was arrested on the train and he was sent to Buchenwald."*

"And then in 1943, my second brother, he was arrested at work and he was transferred to Oranienburg — I think it's near Berlin, and he was hanged there ... his name was Siegfried and he was about 17 or 18 ... it was hard to believe. Why — or how? We didn't know what happened, I mean we didn't know about those concentration camps at all."

A few months after his brother Siegfried's arrest, Burt Romer was taken. "They just came one day and said, 'Get ready. We have to take you away' ... and then (I) packed my little suitcase, it was nighttime, and the next day they took me to a larger city ... and from there — quite a few families had to go with me — they took us to Frankfurt-au-Main, and there they put us in a cattle wagon and closed it overnight, and let us stand there in the way of attacks, and we were standing there and then the air attacks came. And then the next day, I don't know how many cattle cars they connected, and then they took us to Theresienstadt."

That was May 1943. Two years later, Romer was released when the Russians liberated Theresienstadt on May 9, 1945. Through friends, Romer made his way home to be reunited with his father. His brother, Roland, returned from Buchenwald soon thereafter.

Looking back, Romer reflects that he probably never would have left Germany had his mother not been killed. Had that not happened, he says, "I don't think I ever would have come to this country — because I loved her — I was the baby in the family. But after this, I felt I had enough of Germany." Enough so that by January 24, 1948, he was willing to go against his father's wishes and emigrate to the United States.

Soon after he arrived in America, Romer went back to work until he was drafted in 1951. Instead of going to fight in Korea, though, he opted to go to Austria where he became an Army cook. In 1953 he returned to the United States, took a job as a cook in New York, and married Alice Cahn, another survivor he met

---

*NOTE: Buchenwald, one of the most brutal Nazi camps, was established in July 1937 near Weimar, Germany. Of the 238,380 prisoners sent to Buchenwald, 56,549 died there before the camp was liberated by American troops on April 11, 1945. Thousands of others died after being transferred by the Nazis to death camps such as Auschwitz.

before entering the Army. On October 17, 1957, the Romers moved to Greensboro, N.C. because his wife's parents had settled there and because they felt New York City was no place to raise their one child, Helene.

Immediately after the war, Romer was too busy resettling, reuniting with his father, to talk about the Holocaust. Perhaps, he says, he also did not want to become the kind of person his brother turned into after several years in Buchenwald. When Romer talks about his brother, he doesn't even mention his name unless asked, and his normally open approach to telling his story shifts to a low-voiced, strained narrative.

"Him and me are like two different human beings," Romer explains. "Maybe I should mention here the Kristallnacht. He was learning to be a baker; in other words, this is different over there than here; over there you got to learn a profession ... so he was learning the complete bakery business. And in Kristallnacht — his boss man was Jewish — in the Crystal night a Nazi took a spade and hit my brother over the head and his head was split."

Maybe that's why his brother is so bitter, and hard to get along with, Romer says. "He's different," Romer says. "I don't think he's got any feelings for me or anything." His brother's lack of warmth seems to have influenced Romer's own life, which is a quiet study in hard work, family strength and personal fortitude. He told his daughter about the Holocaust when she began to ask questions about her paternal grandmother's fate. But he rarely discusses his experiences with fellow employees at the U.S. Postal Service where he has worked for more than 15 years.

I'll tell you the truth, most of the people I work with, I don't know how to describe this, but it looks to me like they're not interested in discussing things," Romer says.

So Burt Romer is quiet unless someone asks him to speak.

* * *

Other survivors are not so silent. Hearing Elias Mordechai[4], 74, tell his story of survival is more like listening to a speech than suffering through a mournful tale of anguish.*

---

*NOTE: Elias Mordechai died August 20, 1987, at age 78.

He is best at telling what his hometown, Jannina, Greece, was like before the Nazis turned this quiet pastoral village into a town of terror on March 25, 1944. What Elias doesn't remember about that day, his second wife, Esther, 64, recalls vividly.[5] For years, she could not speak so openly. She would cry mid-sentence, lose her train of thought or have nightmares.

"The thing is with me, I'm very emotional," Esther says in her careful English. "He's the one that can talk for 24 hours, and it don't bother him." She points one small olive-skin finger at her husband. He smiles, starts to speak, then is quiet as she hushes him.

"But me, it tears me up to pieces," Esther says. "So I don't like to start over, and over, and over, because, you know, my heart, it eats my heart inside. And I try to forget."

But she will talk about the months she spent in Auschwitz for the right reasons. "Because you're going to do something about it, you're going to put something down and let other people know, you know, what happened."

Elias nods in agreement. When each is interviewed, the other listens, occasionally contributing an insight or forgotten date. The Holocaust, like their roots, is an experience they will always share.

Elias was a young adult when the Greek army drafted him early in the war, in his early 30s when the Nazis consigned his first wife and his 4½-year-old daughter to the death chambers.

Esther was 22, married less than a year, when the Nazis came.

"I married the first time, September 17, 1943. We got married, my brother and I, we got married the same day. Then on a Saturday morning, 1944, like early in the morning, like 7 o'clock, somebody knocked the door so hard and we didn't know what happened, and the Germans was outside. They gave us exactly two hours to get ready. Two of my brothers was begging my mother to go up in the attic and hide. My mother was screaming like anything. She said she not going to leave anybody behind. Everybody — the whole family is going — we was very close. The whole family was going to go together.

"So my two brothers didn't have no choice. So we all got ready. We took a couple of loaves of bread, a quilt or a blanket. And my grandmother had passed away a month ago. And my mother had made a cake for the prayer. When the Germans came in, my mother had it in her hands; and when the Germans came in and push us out of the door, that cake fell in front on the stoop of the house."

Esther Mordechai does not remember anyone warning her or her family of what might happen before the Nazis arrived. "I think it was God's — was the Lord's will for everybody to go just like that. Looked like it was asleep, you know, everybody got their eyes closed and (it) happened all of a sudden.

"But our neighbors across the street — when we got out of the house, and that cake fell in the stoop, and the Germans was pushing my mother to get out of the way, we saw the neighbors across the street coming in with everything, you know. They had thick bags on their shoulders. They knew the night before; but they didn't tell nobody."

Esther is uncertain, but she estimates that Jannina had a population of 2,000 people. Maybe one-third were Jewish, she says, and all the Jews were rounded up on March 25, 1944.

"They took us to a big place and gathered everybody together. And it was like everybody gathered there   all the Jewish people — they had a schedule, you know. Everybody's name was written down. They know how many people was there. And that afternoon they send trucks, like they put horses in, and everybody got in. It was snowing. It was March 25 and it was snowing ... they called the names before they put us in the truck. ... I was, you know, completely lost. You know, I was 22 years old. I said, 'What are they going to do to us? Where are they going to take us?' "

From the years he served in the Greek army, Elias Mordechai was better-informed about what the Nazis did to Jews, but no less confused than Esther about what would actually happen to him, his first wife and child.

"They had taken the Jews and put them in ... one place, and then put them in the back of a truck," he says. "There is no food, nothing and up in the trucks, and went to a little town ... (We were put in) one big building, used to be a warehouse. Two thousand, two thousand people in one building. Is no food, not a thing, no water, no food. After eight days there was a transport. It come — the train. (In) each wagon, 75 kids, families, each wagon. They was called a car. And 75 each ... there was no food ... and taking the train through Yugoslavia, Bulgaria, through Czechoslovakia and stopped the train. Eight days and nights, that train and stopped at Auschwitz, Poland. ... A lot of people have died, you know, in the wagons when this come to Auschwitz."

"Auschwitz ... he stop the trains, he come — the SS, the Nazi with a machine gun and take every woman and child — separate. Everyone over 45, 50 years old, separated. Every young man, strong, looked healthy, to the right and take the families in the line ... nobody knows where they go ... no have a choice. The machine gun — kill you."

When Esther Mordechai arrived at Auschwitz, she recalls, "Everybody was screaming, 'What are they going to do? What are they going to do?' So a big German comes in — two men come in and they take us out of the train. You know, if you sit 10 days in a train, and you don't stretch your feet — a lot of people didn't know how to walk. So they finally — they separated us when we came out of the train. There was two Germans. They put the young people in the right, the old people in the left. Of all my family, one of my brothers come out (of Auschwitz) and me. Everybody went that same night to the gas chambers. And then I asked the German, I said, 'I want to go with my mother,' and he said, 'You cannot go with your mother because she cannot walk. You're going to walk. And you're going to meet them tonight.' So they put them in the train, and we walked. And we never see them again."

Esther lost three siblings, her first husband, her mother and countless other distant relatives to the gas chambers at Auschwitz. Her father had been dead almost 10 years when the Nazis rounded up Jews in Jannina.

Elias never saw his first wife and child again after the night the trains unloaded at Auschwitz and the Nazis sent the able-bodied in one direction and the old, the sick and the helpless children in another to die. No records exist of how many people were gassed, tortured, shot or killed in some other way at Auschwitz, located in southern Poland near the German border. But Auschwitz was the largest and is the most infamous Nazi camp. It is estimated that four million people died there between 1940 and 1945.[6]

Both of the Mordechais survived, they say, because of a combination of determination to live, religious faith and luck. Esther remembers eating rotten potato peelings. Elias used to stick his hand into the dirt and fill his mouth with grass when no other food was available. Once Elias and his brother Solomon, rubbed their faces with snow and ice to redden them. The idea was to look healthy enough to be selected for a Nazi forced-labor program — one way to delay being exterminated.

Although they are second cousins, the Mordechais did not know each other well until after the war ended. When Esther returned to Jannina, she searched for someone in her family, always hoping someone other than her brother had survived. "And I went to my mother's house and got into the door and my house was wrecked; you know, it was like a stable. And when I walked in and didn't see anybody there, I said to myself, 'I didn't have any business to come back here.' But I wanted to make sure. I felt like 'somebody's there.' "

But no one was. Soon after Esther's return, Elias and his brother, Solomon, came home. The brothers ran into Esther and her female cousins. "We was able to get two rooms in my husband's brother's house," Esther says, "and we all live in one place. So everybody had to talk about it, 'They're going to get married, they're going to get married.' "

A few months later they did, on July 6, 1946. Esther remembers wearing the only dress she owned. In 1947, their first daugther, Evelyn, was born. In 1950, the Mordechais moved to Athens. On September 15, 1951, they emigrated to the United States because Esther had relatives in Greensboro. By then, their second daughter, Annie, had been born. With a preschooler and a toddler in tow, the Mordechais arrived in Greensboro. Elias got a job in a pajama factory earning $46 per week.

It took Esther several years to adjust to living in a new country in a strange culture, but she's not sorry she came. Elias has no regrets either. "I believe the greatest people in America," he says adamantly. "People come from all over Europe to build one nation.

"You have to explain for it to never happen again," he says. "I feel better in heart. That means explaining it to many, many, a thousand millions. You have to explain (across) this earth. Never happen again, one crazy leader, he can destroy. Look how many people died. They could die again. Maybe one leader could destroy

In recent years, telling the tale has come somewhat easier for Elias Mordechai, easier because others have broken their silence. He no longer feels he must tell his story alone. "You have brought me back to life," he says. "The earth has to know what happened. One crazy leader can destroy the earth."

He says those same words over and over. They are almost a litany, a plea.

"If you know what happened, you can save the future," Mordechai says. "It helps me much. It is my duty to explain. ... I just feel good because I got people with me. ... In the history, one mistake, it can destroy the earth.'

The small, aging Greek raises one gnarled, worn hand. It is not a fist, but a personal salute to others who join him in making sure that the past will not be repeated.

CHAPTER 2
INSIDE A CONCENTRATION CAMP

It was a rainy October afternoon the first time I met Susan Cernyak-Spatz, Phd. The directions she had given to her Charlotte home were as clear and precise as the even-pitched tone of her voice over the telephone when the appointment was set. Without making a single wrong turn, I veered off Interstate 77 in Charlotte, easily maneuvering the several streets to the condominium complex where she now lives with her husband, Hardy Spatz.

She greeted me before I could even knock. She is a small, sturdy redhead with just a trace of an accent and a quick, warm smile. An aged poodle shuffled at her heels.

It has been a busy day, she explained, as she let me in. "I've just returned from class. We have to walk the dog — she's getting old, you see — before we can sit down and talk. I hope that's all right"[7]

At 62, Susan Cernyak-Spatz is a successful professional, a professor of German and French at the University of North Carolina at Charlotte. She is quick-witted, articulate and specific about why she has made time to talk.

When her three children were small, she discussed her experiences with them, explained what she has been through first in Theresienstadt, then in Auschwitz.

"First of all, not every mother runs around with this thing." Sitting at the table in her kitchen, she points to the number "34042" tattoed on the outside of her lower left forearm. "So they knew about the number, they knew I was a survivor. But don't forget one thing: Until about '63 or so, it wasn't very 'in' to talk about it. People didn't want to know about it."

The media blitz surrounding the trial of Adolf Eichmann* helped change that. "Not until the Eichmann trial did the topic of the Holocaust become interesting," she says. "As a matter of fact, I wrote my dissertation on the German Holocaust literature. When I first told my professor at the University of Kansas that I was writing about the German Holocaust, (it was like) who the hell is interested in that? And at that time, nobody was. My dissertation is being published now after 10 years of being out. Ten or 12 years. At that time, nobody wanted to touch it."

So the education of this generation of young people in the history of the Holocaust may depend on people like her, Cernyak-Spatz seems to be saying. "They should be educated because what we had there, and it becomes more and more obvious, was a group of professionals ..." She stumbles in mid-sentence, changes course, sharpens her emphasis. "What you had was a bureaucratic, organized murder. There was nothing emotional about it, there was nothing over-sadistic, over-anti-Semitic about it. ... This thing was planned down to the detail of how long — how many calories it takes for a man to survive for two-and-one-half years, how much disease to let run rampant to hurry the extermination. I mean, originally Jews were supposed to be all gassed. And the interesting thing is that, if people had believed what Hitler wrote in his famous book, *Mein Kampf,* they would have known, but nobody believed."

Susan Cernyak-Spatz's story is one of survival, a fight to stay alive that began when she was barely a teenager. Her parents were forced to flee from one country to another, seeking respite from Adolf Hitler's growing domination of Europe. It began in 1936. Things had gotten so bad that her father, Ernest Eckstein, decided to take his wife, Friedel, and their one child, Susan (then 13 years old) and leave Berlin where the Ecksteins had lived for eight years.

---

*NOTE: Adolf Eichmann became Hitler's expert on Zionism in 1934. He also became one of the major architects of the death camps as head of the Emigration and Evacuation desk of the Nazi regime. He scheduled, organized and managed the deportation of Jews across Europe to the camps. In 1962, after his capture and trial for genocide, he was put to death in Israel.

"Unfortunately, when my father insisted that we leave Germany, my mother was one of those people that ... had always cherished material things. (She said), 'I don't want to go to a foreign country where I don't speak the language and they won't let me take my things with me.' And that was it. My mother simply did not want to part with her belongings, and so we went to Austria. And, in 1938, Hitler went to Austria. And from Austria we went to Czechoslovakia. Hitler invaded Czechoslovakia in 1939. My father had made arrangements for us to cross the border into Poland and then get out of Poland because we had a branch of our business in Belgium. And my uncle and his family were there. And so father had made the arrangements, and mother said, 'Well, we don't know whether it is safe, so you go first and the child and I will follow.' But unfortunately he went on the 31st of August 1939, the beginning of World War II. That meant he got out of Poland — practically on the last plane — because the blitzkrieg started on September 1.

"And we were stuck. Mother refused to let me go. Some friends of mine wanted me to go on a transport to Israel. There were some illegal transports to Israel at the time. And I met some of those friends a couple of years ago, who had gone with that transport. They had suffered a lot on their trip. But they got through. But my mother refused to let me go. And so, in 1942, in Czechoslovakia, the Czech Jews began to be deported. They deported them first into the Polish ghettos. And then, into the ghetto Theresienstadt in Czechoslovakia. We were deported to Theresienstadt from Prague. My mother, due to some personal decisions, chose to go on a further transport. So mother chose at that time, to be deported east from Theresienstadt, and nobody knew where to. Well, we found out later — unfortunately found out — (I saw her name on the transport list when I worked in the political department in Auschwitz) — that she arrived on the transport but never came into the camp. So probably, I would say, that at that age — mother was 45 — she was one of the fortunate ones. Because, at her age, she would have come into the camp and she would have suffered terribly and then gone into the gas. This way, she went into the gas, not knowing what was happening, not knowing what was going on."

Susan Cernyak-Spatz remained in Theresienstadt until January 1943, when she was sent to Auschwitz, where she remained until 1945. "If you, how should I say, foiled them, so to speak, and somehow survived the obligatory two-and-one-half months which you were given as survival time, according to their project, you had a better chance. ... Strange as it might seem, there was a hierarchy of social standing in camp just as much as there was in life, and the lower your number, the longer you survived, the higher your standing. And the one advantage I had when I came to Auschwitz was that I spoke both fluent German and fluent Czech. The Jewish camp administration, the Jewish camp leader, the block administrators, the block servants, everyone was Czech. I mean Slovakian. The language is pretty similar. And, if you could communicate with them, you had one leg up already. They did not like to speak German, so speaking Czech was to your advantage.

"One of the things that probably started me out on a career intermittently in Auschwitz was that on the first day of walking out on the outside of the commando, not knowing the rules and regulations of the camp, I just acted on instinct. We were standing in line by the gate waiting to march out, and there was the work commander leader, an SS man, and I just blithely stepped up and said to him, 'Reporting name so-and-so, number so-and-so, and I'm a secretary.' And that man's mouth fell open because nobody had dared to do that, and somehow I suppose I must have made an impression. He wrote my number down, and everybody in line said: 'My God, he wrote your number down, you're going to go to the gas.' But three days later, myself and some other people (who) had given their profession as secretary were called to work in the political department, to serve as temporaries. I guess they had a lot of investigations down there and they needed people to take the transcripts of the investigations. And through that, after about two weeks or three weeks, I got a job in the political department, which was the elite department, clean and relatively well-fed. And you could wash and what have you. I was in the main Auschwitz camp. But after about a month or so, somebody in the secretarial commando was caught smuggling information out of a file, probably out of a personal file. Like in all jobs, last hired, first fired. The example was made with myself and two others that were on the bottom rung. And we were kicked out of Auschwitz and back to Birkenau to the extermination camp. And then I made my way through typhoid fever, scurvy, hepatitis, and the whole bit. Well, I survived."

The question she has the most trouble answering is how she survived. "No, No," she says, "Not religious faith, I'm sorry to say. I'm an observant Jew, but religious faith had absolutely nothing to do with it. I've never been an unobservant Jew, but I've never been Orthodox. I come from a Reform Jewish family, but faith had nothing to do with it. It was, I think, two things: First, I suppose, a certain genetic predisposition to be able to survive disease. I don't know. Secondly, and to me that's one of the most important things, I believe a lot of people when they came into Birkenau, which was a surrealistic nightmare situation, couldn't accept the fact that they were there. Why were they there? They couldn't live like that. No normal being could live like that. They totally refused to adapt or even attempt to cope within the frame of that nightmare. And, I think, if I remember, from the very first day on, whether it was walking around in Russian prisoners' uniforms, and with a shaved head, and with one bowl for eating and elimination and everything, I accepted it. I accepted it and I manipulated to cope with anything, and I think that that was one of the most important things, that you accepted the frame of the situation and lived from one minute to the next, or from one day to the next, with no other aim but survival.

"Because I have seen people who simply would lie down and die because life like that's not worth living. And, just like today where the physician will tell you your own mental condition was part of your cure, it was the same thing there. Your mental condition was part of your survival. Survival was the utmost thing and survival needed to be within the frame of that given world. That was the world I live in."

It was also a world in which building a support group was a prerequisite to survival. Stories of one prisoner's kindness to another abound in the history of survivors. Even more common, though, are stories of constantly changing allegiances, experiences in which survival depended more upon keeping tabs on who was running things than it did on making friends.

"You always had to have a support group," Cernyak-Spatz says. "The support group might change because any time you change commandoes, or change jobs, or change blocks, you had to have a new support group. ... Anybody who tells you that he existed by himself, especially in the lower commandoes, is lying. You had to have a support group."

A twist of fate and the cowardice of the SS officers who guarded her also may have ensured her survival. After being evacuated from Auschwitz by the Germans in January 1945, Cernyak-Spatz was placed in a group of 25 women and taken to Ravensbruck, a women's concentration camp north of Berlin.

"Maybe it was just that the SS were basically cowards, not only cowards, but they were shirkers, because most of these SS men stayed in these concentration camps as guardsmen and administrators, because they didn't want to go to the front," she says scornfully. "So our heroes, our three heroes of our commando, decided they didn't want to go to the front just before the war ended. So they invented a job, a commando for us, 25 girls. We stayed in Ravensbruck and didn't do anything. For the next three months, we just created the protection for our commando leaders so they didn't have to go to the front.

"April 28, we evacuated from Ravensbruck. But at that time, the concentration camp prisoners had become pretty valuable assets, because it was at that time that the Germans had some kind of arrangement to exchange their prisoners of war for concentration camp prisoners. And the Allies insisted that the first concentration camp prisoners they wanted were women. That was certainly gallant."

Cernyak-Spatz was among the last of the women to leave. When the Red Cross evacuated prisoners by nationalities, she refused to leave with either the Germans or the Austrians, two groups she could have joined. "But I was rather stubborn because my group of 25 were mostly Czechoslovakian girls. ... I insisted on remaining loyal to my friends. From Ravensbruck, we went sort of northwest and we ended up in a little town called Malchow and we came upon — I would say, if I looked at a map — the area exactly where the Russians and the Americans met. We had been marching for two days and nights. ... And I think, it must have been on — I think the day that Hitler died — I remember one morning we woke up on the meadow there and a motorcycle came by and someone screamed, 'The Fuhrer is dead!' So everybody, of course, knew. The Germans, their faces fell, and our faces, of course, lit up. And we marched on.

"You have to visualize. It seemed on those highways that all of Germany was marching west. Because they were so petrified of the Russians that they were running. ... All of a sudden a vehicle came east and from afar all we could see was sort of a khaki-colored, sort of blunt snout of a vehicle with a white star on it. And everybody said, 'My God, the Russians, the Russians, we ran right into the Russians.' Because the Germans kept telling us, 'We will get you away from the Russians because the Russians rape and the Russians murder.' Of course, the Russians rape and murder, because that's what they (the Germans) did to them in Russia. So, anyway, everybody was petrified. So this vehicle comes close. And I see on the top of the side of that vehicle, which I didn't know was a jeep, written 'Daisy Mae.' But I had never seen a jeep. There was a man in uniform, and on the back of that jeep sat a guy in a concentration camp prisoner's uniform. So we stopped them. ... I walked up the guy and said, 'Would you please help us?' And he said, 'What the hell language are you talking?' And I said, 'I'm talking English as far as I know.' He said, 'Well, why should I help you? You're a German.' I said, 'We're not German, and rolled up the sleeve (to show him her concentration camp number).'" The concentration camp prisoner sitting on the jeep backed up her claim.

Cernyak-Spatz remembers that the other prisoner said, " 'Those kids are from Auschwitz. Those are concentration camp prisoners.' And this, G.I., I guess he was a corporal, said, 'Look, we can't do anything for you right now. We got lost from our outfit. During the advance of our outfit, we got lost and we don't know where the hell we are.' I said, 'But can't you do something to let the (German) guards know the war is over?' He said, 'I'll tell you what. Tell him (the guard) to hand over that submachine gun.' And I walked up to the guard and most politely said, 'Would you mind handing over the submachine guns?' He said, 'Are you crazy?' I said, 'Those are Americans, and they would like your submachine guns.' "

To the delight of the liberated prisoners, the German guard relinquished his gun. The American soldier told Cernyak-Spatz and other former prisoners to make their way to the next town where the soldier believed they would find a group of American forces.

"They had told us to go on to the next town. But the Americans were not there. Several of us were thinking of staying there, but we were urged to go to the American lines. We set out again and got caught in artillery fire."

After managing to get through the artillery fire unharmed, the liberated prisoners eventually came upon a group of German refugees and moved on to an American checkpoint. "Again, we went through the same bit." Cernyak-Spatz and her small band of former prisoners finally convinced officials that they were **not** Germans, and Cernyak-Spatz found the American assistance for which she had been searching.

"It was more or less anti-climatic," she remembers. "It was rather strange. That little town. ... And I remember walking down the street and thinking: 'Nobody stops me. I can walk as long as I want on this street and nobody is going to stop me. Nothing.' That was when it really sank into me ... that I was really free."

With American help, she made her way to a displaced persons camp but did not stay long. "I started working for the American Counter Intelligence Corps detachment of the camp as an interpreter, and the miracle, I would say, happened at that time, in the Hagenau displaced persons camp. One of the officers of the CIC detachment was a Jewish man who had emigrated from Germany to England and then to America before the war began. One day I was talking to him and asked him where he was from in Germany.

"Berlin," he said. Then she asked the crucial question.

"And I said, 'I know Berlin is a large city and there were close to 500,000 Jews there. But, just by sheer coincidence, did you by any chance know anybody in the clothing manufacturing business by the name of Schuermann?' He looked at me strangely and said, 'You mean Julius Schuermann or Louis Schuermann? They are my cousins.' I decided to press my luck further. 'By any chance, at the Schuermanns' — either at Julius' house or at Louis' house did you ever run into anybody by the name of Eckstein?' 'But of course,' he said, 'I played bridge with them. Mr. Eckstein is in Brussels, but his wife and his child died in Auschwitz.' "

Cernyak-Spatz set the record straight. "The child is right here," she said. That's how she found out that her father was alive. The young lieutenant wired his cousin, Louis Schuermann in London, who wired Cernyak-Spatz's uncle in New York. He, in turn, wired her father in Brussels, who had also given up all hope of ever seeing his family again.

After working in the summer of 1945 for the American and then the British military government as an interpreter, Susan Cernyak-Spatz joined her father in Brussels in August 1945. Back then, miracles did sometimes happen.

CHAPTER 3
LEAVE-TAKING AT KRISTALLNACHT

November 9, 1938. Across Nazi Germany, German Jews watch in incredulity as their relatives are beaten, their synagogues burned and the windows of their stores are shattered by rocks. The destruction, organized by gangs of anti-Semitic Germans, occurs with the blessing of Nazi propaganda minister, Joseph Paul Goebbels, and with the cooperation of local German police. So many store windows are broken, so much glass litters the streets that Jews call the night "Kristallnacht", literally "Glass Night" or the "Night of Shattered Glass."

After Kristallnacht, the insurance claims filed by Jews for property damage in the form of broken windows came to six million marks.[8] But Nazi authorities refused to accept the claims, forced Jews to pay for the damages and repairs themselves. Goebbels, who issued the initial call for demonstrations against Jews, saw the destruction as proper retribution for the death of Ernst Von Rath, a minor official at the German embassy in Paris. Von Rath was fatally wounded by an angry young Jew, Herschel Grynszpan, after Grynszpan's father told his son of being herded onto trains with 15,000 other Jews deported to Poland late in 1938.[9]

Walter Falk, a 56-year-old salesman who now lives in Greensboro, remembers Kristallnacht as the beginning of the end. He was 11 years old in 1938.[10]

"A fellow by the name of Herschel Grynszpan shot a German I believe the man was not the ambassador, but he was an attache at

25

the German embassy in Paris. ... Seems the Nazis had just been waiting for something like this and they decided to take revenge on the Jews that night and on the tenth of November."

"My mother and I lived in an apartment in Karlsruhe and we didn't know what was going on. The first thing I noticed as I went to school that morning was that the Jewish shoe store downstairs had all its windows smashed. The glass and shoes were all over the street."

"I went off to school, and the first thing we were told in school was that the teacher would be late because the synagogue was burning and that the teacher, a religious man, had gone over to the synagogue to save the Torah, which he did. He brought it out of the burning synagogue, I was told, and then came over to school."

The next hour was uneventful, a brief peace. "Then some plainclothesmen, I guess they were from the Gestapo, came and they took the teacher and the headmaster away, and I went home.

"Getting home, I found my mother in tears because two men had been up to our apartment and searched it. They had torn the curtains and a few pictures off the wall. I suppose they were looking for valuables. There were looking (to see) if there was a safe behind the picture. My mother was very upset."

Nelly, Falk's mother, was a widow. His father had died after serving in World War I. They lived alone in Karlsruhe.

"My mother said, 'Let's go to Grandma's,' and that's what we did. We went to the railroad station and took the train. My Grandma lived about an hour and a half away in Gondelsheim, a small village. Everything was in order there. There was a Nazi in full uniform standing in front of Grandma's house; he happened to be the next-door neighbor. This man put on his Nazi uniform and stood in front of the house so that no one would do anything to Grandma. He looked out for us. ... So he was a good Nazi, if there is such a thing."

Falk, a dark-haired man of medium height, shakes his head as he tells the story. It is an ironic twist in an otherwise bitter tale of survival.

Like many other Jewish children, Falk had experienced the gradual erosion of his rights after Hitler came to power in 1933.

was not permitted to say 'Heil Hitler' or wear a uniform. This set me apart from the rest of my classmates. I had to attend school parades and listen to propaganda speeches. The attitude towards Jews became worse as time went on. The other students were told not to socialize with Jews. The teachers were not supposed to speak to Jewish parents. In 1937, the Jewish children were separated from other German children, and we were placed into a school with abnormal children. On one side of the building were the Jewish kids, and on the other side were the handicapped and retarded children."

By 1938, Falk was a member of a Jewish Zionist organization. The group leader suggested to many in the organization that they emigrate. " 'You better get the heck out of here,' he said," Falk recalls. "He was going to Palestine, and I made an application to go to Palestine."

After the events of Kristallnacht and the slowly worsening conditions in her mother's small village, Nelly Falk did not object. Falk applied to emigrate to Palestine. He also applied to emigrate to England because a family friend living there wrote and offered to arrange transportation for him.

"I said I'd go to whatever place I could go first," Falk says. "And, now after the tenth of November, my mother was more than willing to send me out. She wanted me out."

Falk did not object to leaving his mother behind, but went along with her wishes when she insisted he go to England early in 1939. "She said, 'Yes, I'll come, too,' She wanted to come. As a matter of fact, she applied for an exit visa. She got it a few days before the war started. It was no good to her.

"After I left Germany, my mother moved in with her mother in the village of Gondelsheim. On October 22, 1940, all the Jews in this part of Germany, which was the province called Baden, were deported to Vichy, France. They were not told where they were going. They were given 15 minutes — at most, two hours — to get a suitcase packed and they were allowed to take, I think, 50 kilos — or whatever they could carry. There were little children and there were very old people. There were sick people. ... There were no exceptions made. They were put into cattle cars and sent off. My mother and grandmother were sent to Camp De Gurs, which was in unoccupied Vichy, France. My grandmother, I was told, left home without her teeth."

Falk grimaces at the bitter recollection. He learned what he now knows about his mother's and his grandmother's fates by searching for answers after the war. His grandmother survived until 1944 in the camp in France, but she died before being liberated.

"In 1942, my mother was sent to Auschwitz."

He opens the book he has brought with him. A thick volume, it lists the intricate, macabre records which the Nazis kept of deportations.

'It says here — Nelly Falk shipped on Convoy #33, September 16, 1942. The Germans were very good at keeping records and they listed exactly the train she was on. And she was identified by her birthdate. There was only one Nelly Falk listed who was born on July 1, 1899. So there is no question about this."

So she definitely was gassed? Falk, normally painstakingly responsive and cooperative, frowns at the question. "Yes, yes, yes, yes," he says, nodding his head with each affirmative answer.

After leaving Germany for the children's home in England where he lived for the duration of the war, Falk never saw his mother or his grandmother again.

'I have a few letters. As long as France was not occupied, my mother could send a few letters. But they were very few and far between. And, to be honest, I didn't realize what was going on and Mother didn't realize what was going on. She didn't believe that her life was in danger.

"Very few — very few people tried to escape. There were opportunities to escape, and I know of two couples who did escape. One husband and wife decided to go, and they did. They crossed the Pyrenees and they made it to Switzerland, where they were interned (in a concentration camp), and spent the rest of the war in a Swiss camp. I was only 14- or 15-years-old and didn't understand what the Nazis were up to."

Falk emigrated to the United States in 1944, coming to New York to live with an aunt. He finished high school there and was drafted to serve with the American forces during the Korean War

He lives in a quiet residential neighborhood in Greensboro with his wife, Ginger. She also is a German immigrant, but her family left Germany before the war. The Falks, who have no children, moved to Greensboro in 1960 because Walter Falk's sales region is North Carolina and Virginia.

Falk says it was years before he learned to relinquish his bitterness and hate. "They were my feelings. It's just recently that I could talk about it. I would never have talked about the Holocaust during 1940 and 1950 and maybe into the '60s· I couldn't talk about it. It was too fresh. But now it needs to be told."

"Because there are people. ... who say it never happened, and there are also people today, if you listen to them carefully, who are trying to justify what happened. For instance, I listened to a German television show. And they said, 'Yeah, all right, we did this to the Jews, but look what the Allies did to Germany. Look what they did to Dresden, and look what they did to Hamburg. They bombed these cities and they killed 20,000 civilians.' They say one equates the other, but it doesn't. My mother was helpless and wouldn't hurt a fly. Two wrongs don't make a right."

There is anguish in Walter Falk's eyes. He keeps talking, but there is little left to say. He made it clear at the start of the interview that he doesn't think of himself as a survivor. "I didn't go through what other people with numbers on their arms went through."

As it ends, a quiet smile returns to his face. No, he says, he has no complaints. North Carolina is a beautiful state with friendly people. Greensboro is a pretty city.

"I'm the luckiest fellow in the world," Falk says. "It could have been me down there, too. No, I am very lucky."

CHAPTER 4
IN HIDING

What Shelly Weiner remembers best about the 18 months she was in hiding during World War II is that her Aunt Sophie and her mother told stories to amuse two frightened Jewish pre-schoolers.[11] Stashed away in a small attic-like space in the top of a Polish farmer's barn, Weiner and her cousin Raya and their mothers were hiding from the Nazis.

"I don't remember too much about it," Weiner says. "I don't even know how we spent our day. I know we couldn't stand up ... we had to lay. Most of (the time) we were flat."

"We told stories. My mother and aunt would tell a story and we would all fantasize. There were no toys; there were no games; there was no exercise."[12]

It wasn't much of a life for a bright-eyed, brown-haired little girl, once surrounded by family and friends in her hometown of Rovno, Poland. Born Rachel Weiner (she later changed her name to Rochelle), Shelly Weiner was used to the comraderie at her mother's grocery store and her grandfather's flour mill. Once the war began, loneliness and fear were her companions.

But a life of hiding was better than no life. So Shelly Weiner, her mother Eva, her Aunt Sophie, and her cousin Raya, lived that way for better than a year and a half during the war. They were far better off than most of the Jews of Poland. Of the more than 20 European nations occupied by the Nazis during the war, Poland had the largest Jewish community. An estimated 3.3 million Jews

The statistic is a figure that Shelly Weiner recalls with a grimace. The grimace returns to her face again and again as she thinks back four decades to her experiences as a terrified little girl.

"I think what I remember the most were the frightening experiences that we had," she says. "I don't remember the everyday things that were going on."

The details of everyday existence that she does recall are snatches of a past she has claimed in conversations with her mother. Eva Weiner, 67, is a soft-spoken woman, who speaks of the war in a tight voice, strangled with emotion.*

In a joint interview with her daughter about their days in hiding, Eva Weiner says she will never forget the night she learned the Nazis were marching to Rovno, a city about 60 miles from the Soviet-Polish border.

"That's the worst thing," she says. "My daughter was three years old, and I was packing her things to send her to camp.[13] That Saturday night I was sitting and sewing in the labels (in clothes), and my brother came in and said, 'Don't send her.' She (Shelly) was the first baby in the family ... the baby grandchild."

Eva Weiner's brother, David, made it clear why he had come. He said he was entering the Polish army, and that he wanted to warn Eva that the political situation in Poland was changing rapidly. His real message was clear, too. Don't send Shelly away, not even 15 or 16 miles to the site of the summer camp Eva had planned for her daughter to attend. It just would not be safe.

Eva remembers the people of Rovno still did not expect the worse. "We was hoping it's (not) going to be (long before) the war finished, and everybody's going to come back home, and we'll be back in Poland like we used to be."

But a week after my brother left, the Nazis invaded. "They came in and they took out from our city 500 men. The first night I'll never forget, if I can talk about it. And they took them, they said they taking them to work, and they took them outside the city and they — killed them ... Then when the Germans killed the 500 people, they started to make believe they going to be good to the Jews, and they make the committee, and they make Jewish police

---

*NOTE: Eva and Shelly Weiner have the same last name because Shelly also married a man named Weiner.

31

and they make this ... Everyday was something else. One day they wanted Jews should bring them the best clothes; one day the Jews should bring them the rings, and the gold, and the diamonds. And if they find something in somebody's house, these people would all be killed."

Before the German invasion, three of Weiner's uncles and her father Meyer were drafted into the Russian army, the beginning of the end of the Orthodox Jewish family life into which Weiner and her parents, Eva and Meyer, had been born.

"The Germans attacked in June 1940 and came to Rovno in August," Shelly Weiner says. "The first thing the Germans did was very typical. They made all Jews wear the Yellow Stars and there were many other restrictions. The men were taken immediately.

"My grandfather had five sons; we lived in a courtyard all together. The first incident that I recall at that time that was frightening was as follows: We had a big barn in the back of the compound. We made a hiding place in this barn, and the men would spend their days there but they would come to the houses for meals. My cousin Raya ... and I would be playing outside and we would be the lookouts. So if we saw a jeep with the SS coming down, we would run and warn them and the men would run back to the barn and hide."[14]

The Germans invaded Soviet Poland in June 1941. They came to Rovno in August. After the initial roundup and brutal shooting deaths, the people of Rovno had even more to fear. In a city of probably 80,000 to 100,000 citizens, there were perhaps 15,000 Jews, Weiner estimates. Many had lived in Rovno for generations. But the Nazis soon split up close families like Weiner's when German soldiers began rounding up Jews for slave labor camps.

Then, in the winter of 1940-41, the Nazis herded the city's remaining Jews into the ghetto, following a pattern they used across Europe and particularly in Poland. Crammed into living quarters meant for far fewer people, life in the ghetto was hard, provisions sparse and comforts few. It also could be dangerous.

"My mother and I were in the ghetto for about three months. I remember being very frightened because the quarters were very close. We were very closely watched. We were not even allowed to go outside. One time, I did go outside and a soldier pointed a gun at me; so I never went outside again. We were there about three months and we heard rumors that there was going to be another roundup. Although I do not know exactly how it was arranged, we managed to escape."[15]

Eva Weiner remembers that her husband found out the Germans planned to take the sick and the old people from the ghetto and kill them. She was ill with typhus at the time. "So right away, they put me in a horse and wagon — and her (Shelly) and they sent us to my sister."[16]

That sister, Aunt Sophie to Shelly, lived in a small village about 12 kilometers from Rovno. She had arranged with a farmer to hide Shelly, Eva, Raya (Shelly's cousin) and herself. There were several reasons for the farmer agreed to take such a risk. His son was a resistance fighter, deeply involved in the Polish Underground. The son also had a special fondness for Shelly's aunt, who had been kind to him when was a young child. Most importantly, the four terrified Jews paid the farmer and his wife for their trouble.

The two women and two girls first hid in a small space in the top of the farmer's barn. It was large enough only for them to sit or lie down. Their Polish friends made a tunnel through which they brought food to the hidden Jews. After about 18 months, informers alerted the Nazis to their hiding place and the four decided to make a run for it, taking off into the woods. They spent a sleepless night in the forest listening to the sounds of Nazis searching for them. The next day another farmer came to their aid. He had known Eva Weiner back in the days when she ran the small grocery store in Rovno. He also was a friend of the first farmer who had befriended the Weiners. The second farmer took the two frightened women and their terrified daughters into wheat fields near his home where they spent three days hiding until the Nazis tired of their search.

"The next hiding place was under a trough where horses drank," Shelly Weiner says. "We lay there, but it was too horrible and we couldn't take it. My mother said she would rather die than continue living there."[17]

After several weeks under the trough, the Weiners found another place to hide when their second farmer friend moved them to an underground tunnel where he stored his grains.

"And that was where we lived for three months," Shelly Weiner says. "It was pretty bad because there was one hole that he dug for air and in order to get the food we would have to crawl on our bellies through a tunnel. Our living conditions were damp, dark and frightening. Just candles and lots of rats."[18]

The farmer was their only contact with the outside world during those three months. Although they did not know of other Jews who were hidden, Shelly Weiner remembers being told of a relative who had been in hiding, but was captured by the Germans. And she will never forget the screams she heard coming from nearby fields. Jews and resistance fighters, hidden in the same area near Shelly, screamed as they were captured and tortured by the Nazis.

Only in February 1944 when the Russians took control of Rovno and surrounding areas did Shelly and Eva Weiner emerge from their hiding place.

Both have tried to forget what Rovno was like when they returned. They hate to remember the bombing of the town in the nine months before the war finally ended, the friends and relatives they discovered were gone forever, the loss of almost everything they had known and loved. Until late 1945, they also did not know what had happened to Shelly's father, Meyer.

In 1945, Josef Stalin decreed that all Polish citizens living in the Ukraine could go to Poland now that the Ukraine again was Russian territory. Shelly and her mother left for Poland. There they found Meyer Weiner. Several months later, the trio sneaked across the Polish/German border to the section of Germany then occupied by the United States. After three years in a displaced persons camp, they emigrated to America in 1949 and settled in Philadelphia.

Four decades later, Shelly Weiner looks nothing like the frightened waif who hid from the Nazis. At 47, she is a small, well-clad brunette with enormous brown eyes, slightly olive-hued skin and short, stylishly coiffed hair. Even her accent gives no hint of her Polish roots. Eva Weiner still speaks English haltingly. She is a friendly, softly feminine woman with wavy blond hair. Each gives the other credit for her survival.

Shelly nods her head decisively in her mother's direction when

Till today, she keep — This is my whole life."

Shelly Weiner moved to North Carolina in 1972 with her husband Frank and their children. Her mother and father followed in 1977. Weiner says she came because her husband was working in a high-pressure job in the Northeast and both of them yearned for a simpler, quieter life.

Eva Weiner rarely talks about the Holocaust. For Shelly, talking about it has become one way to cope with it. But she keeps her discussion general when she speaks in public school classrooms or to civic groups. She shies from recalling the nightmares that still plague her and is comfortable with only a brief recitation of her memories.

The main reason that she discusses what she lived through at all is that firsthand accounts of the Holocaust have more impact. "When you read about something in a book, it's entirely different from when you meet a person face to face and you realize that they've got two hands, two arms, two eyes and they're very much like you. And that they have the same rights — the same right to exist as anybody in this world."[19]

Weiner revealed her experiences to her three grown children very gradually. She told them more and more of her story as the youngsters studied the Holocaust in Hebrew School and picked up information from other sources.

Although deeply moved, Weiner says her youngest daughter, Julie, did not feel that she had any real understanding of the Holocaust until the past couple of years. "She couldn't really identify, but she didn't want to toss the whole thing off and pretend it didn't affect her at all," Weiner says.

Weiner decided to take her daughter to Washington, D.C. in April 1983 for a gathering of Holocaust survivors. Her husband, Frank, flew in from New York City where he was working to join his wife and daughter.

The family went out to lunch after the meeting of survivors. As they sat around a table discussing the experience, Shelly Weiner said she began to fully understand the victory of the meeting represented.

"We said, 'You know as bad as it was forty years ago, look what these people were able to accomplish.' I mean, that is incredible, that people who had gone through these horrible things should all be alive, and not only that, but willing to go on with their lives and produce children. That all of them are well-educated, professional well adjusted. It's a triumph of humanity   They didn't win in the end."

"They" are the Nazis. In surviving and living, Shelly Weiner ceased being a victim and joined the ranks of the victors.

CHAPTER 5
LAND WHERE FREEDOM RINGS

In rough and sometimes confusing English that garbles the story he is trying to tell, Anatoly Kizhnerman[20] takes a verbal journey back almost 45 years to his childhood. It is 1941. He is 5 and terrified by conditions in the Jewish ghetto in which he and his family have been placed.

Born in Russia, Kizhnerman moved as a preschooler to the Ukraine. He went with his parents, Anchel and Polina, and his brother, Vladimer. His sister, Rita, was born in the Ukraine a couple of weeks before World War II began.

"As you know, the war between Germany and Russia started June 22, 1941. It was started very unusually because nobody expect the war," Kizhnerman says, slowly trying to paint a historical picture and a backdrop for his story. "And before the war, my parents moved to the Ukraine. ... And in a couple of days, when the war started, the Germans were in the same city where I was living. It is Zmerinka.

"And, of course, most people didn't have time to leave the city. And, second, you know ... the Ukraine was many times invaded by Germany before the Bolshevik revolution time. And Jewish people (who often had suffered at the hands of the Russian military) had the opinion that German soldiers were very nice to Jews. You have to remember, the Ukraine was one of the most nationalistic and anti-Semitic republics in the U.S.S.R. And Jews suffered a lot from the Ukrainian people, too."

So when the German occupation started, many Jews did not try to leave because they didn't believe the information about the

Germans published by the Soviet media. Many Jews, Kizhnerman recalls, believed the Soviets simply were publishing propaganda. Other Jews, he says, did not leave because they could not go elsewhere. The Kizhnermans were luckier than many who remained, even though the Germans herded the family into a soon-overflowing ghetto in Zmerinka.

"The war started on June 22 and the first Germans arrived a few days later. They divided the city into two parts. Under the agreement between Germany and Romania, which was a satellite of Germany, part of the Ukraine had to belong to Romania. And all the Jews living in the Romanian part (including the Kizhnermans) were put in a ghetto. In the other part of the city, all Jews were killed."

Though just a child, Kizhnerman remembers the ghetto well.

"I remember everything. Because, you know, when you're at this age, I was about 5 years old, and you see the terrible things when people can kill each other for a piece of bread because they don't have more to eat, when parents see how their children are dying because they don't have enough to eat."

When one sees such horrible things, he says, even a child remembers them.

"It's very deep in your memory. And you saw everything. And a child's memory keeps very well."

A child who sees what Kizhnerman saw also learns quickly. There is little time for emotion, no room for pity.

"Every human being," he explains, "anyone, animals, when you see something which is dangerous, you will try to protect yourself. ... You saw how people were killed. You saw how the German soldiers looked, how they killed people. And, of course, you develop an attitude by which you protect yourself. And, as a child, you do the same. When you see a soldier, you would try to escape."

Of course, one couldn't really escape from the ghetto. But Kizhnerman soon realized that his best plan of action when lived. In Spring 1940, 160,000 Jews in Lodz were sealed off. In November, nearly 500,000 were forced behind walls and guarded gates in Warsaw.[21]

The Jewish historian Emanuel Ringelblum wrote in his diary on November 8, 1940: "We are returning to the Middle Ages."[22]

In fact, things were much worse. Unlike the ghettos of the Middle Ages, which were places from which Jews could come and go as they pleased, from insular, but happy communities, the Nazi ghettos were miserable places. Hotbeds of disease, the ghettos were overcrowded and the site of forced labor, constant hunger, and often death.[23]

Most alien to Anatoly Kizhnerman was being singled out, moved into an area where other citizens did not come. "When I was a child, most of my friends were non-Jewish boys and girls," he recalls. "And, you know, we didn't feel different. I didn't see a difference between being a Jew or a non-Jew."

As events beyond their control drastically altered life in the Ukrainian section of the U.S.S.R., so did the Kizhnermans' existence change. When the Nazis invaded, Anatoly Kizhnerman's mother was pregnant with his sister, Rita. His mother was a housekeeper. His father worked as a foreman in a sewing factory. The second day after the German invasion began, Anchel Kizhnerman was drafted into the Red Army. He was killed in December 1941, just six months after the Germans came into the Ukraine. His wife lived on, struggling to support three tiny children alone.

"When ... they put us into the ghetto, adults they used for labor to work on their roads, to fix the bridges which were destroyed during the invasion, and which were destroyed by the Soviet Army when they left."

Survival was paramount. "It was not legal," Anatoly Kizhnerman remembers, "but you would exchange your clothes for a meal, for food. And that was the only way to try and survive. Our house, a three-bedroom house, was (crowded)." After the invasion, six families, including the Kizhnermans, squeezed into the same home, somehow managing to fit 20 people into a house meant for five.

"It was only a place to sleep," Kizhnerman says, "but our house had a big garden and we had a lot of vegetables, and this gave us the opportunity to survive. We ate potatoes, I remember. It's all we got.

"And another thing, which was a little bit helpful to us. A lot of Romanian Jews were transferred from Romania to our ghetto."

So the Romanian government sent food and other subsistence to the Jews from their nation, which the Romanian Jews, in turn, shared with their fellow prisoners.

But that sharing could not stave off starvation forever.

"Again, I say, if you will put a person in this situation, his only thought is to survive."

Kizhnerman's family managed for three years until their ghetto was liberated in April 1944 by the Soviet Army. Before the Soviets arrived, though, the Germans again took over the part of Zmerinka that had been controlled by the Romanians. By then, only 300 of 3,000 Jews in the ghetto at the beginning of the war were still alive, Kizhnerman says. The Germans, following a policy they used in concentration camps and other areas immediately before liberation, set out to destroy the Jews still alive. As the Allies advanced and the Nazis retreated, more Jews died.

"And all the Jews, they started, I don't know how they found out, but somebody ... the non-Jewish people, they told the Jews that the Germans were starting to prepare to kill the Jews."

Even the Ukrainian nationals who once helped the Nazis kill Jews now assisted their Jewish neighbors. "This day when somebody gave a message (of) orders to kill the Jews on that night, everybody left the ghetto," Kizhnerman says. "And every family around the ghetto, they started to save the Jews. I remember when we started to run, somebody started to shoot at us. I told my mom, 'Don't worry. Run. Faster. Faster.' "

His memory of the ensuing days is blurry. He recalls that his mother finally found a family willing to hide them until the Soviet soldiers arrived. When the war ended, the Kizhnermans again were Soviet citizens.

Anatoly Kizhnerman, a thoughtful fellow with a quiet smile and a gentle demeanor, says he never really had a childhood before or after World War II.

"After the war, my mama, with three children, small children,

"After the war when I finished high school, I left for Leningrad, I was accepted to ... Radiopolytechnical College, where I majored in designing and manufacturing equipment for electronics industries." There he also met his wife, Rachel, another survivor who lived out the war in hiding in Poland. The Kizhnermans, who have one grown son, Jerry, remained in Leningrad from 1951 until 1980. Anatoly Kizhnerman sought further training, studying to be an engineer.

In spite of some discrimination, being Jewish had little impact on Kizhnerman's life as a Soviet citizen. "I am not a religious person. My being this way, I didn't feel any differentiation between Jew and non-Jew. ... In Russia, we don't call 'Jew' a religious group; it's a nationality."

But being Jewish did mean working harder. To succeed, he says, one had to be the best.

Political events in the Soviet Union worried Kizhnerman, though, who often talked of emigrating to the United States with his wife. "The first reason, because my wife's relatives, all, they live in the United States. And the second reason, it is, you know that by now the U.S.S.R. had started the war in Afghanistan. People in the U.S.S.R., they disagreed about the invasion because they know what it is like suffering from war and what being invaded (means)."

Unlike the thousands of Soviet Jews who applied to emigrate early in the 1980s and were turned down, Kizhnerman was lucky. "First of all, at this time, you know, U.S.S.R. was preparing for the Olympic games. They tried to clean the big cities ... Leningrad, Moscow, Kiev of people which disagree with the Soviet system."

When he and co-workers were questioned by the KGB, Kizhnerman was asked if he had access to information used to design military weapons. "And, of course, I did. But my boss was my best friend and he said I did not."

That vote of confidence, coupled with looser policies on Jewish emigration at the time, enabled the Kizhnermans to leave. They came to the United States in 1980, stopping briefly in Philadelphia to take an intensive course in English. In March 1981, they moved to Greensboro, where Rachel Kizhnerman's aunt and cousin, Eva and Shelly Weiner, lived.

Anatoly Kizhnerman still has mixed feelings about his adopted homeland. He rarely encounters overt anti-Semitism. But his work as an engineer does bring him into contact with people prejudiced against Jews. Most disturbing, he says, are neo-Nazis and the fact that American law allows such groups to exist.

You know, the United States is a great country. A lot of people, they study about the history of World War II. We know how dangerous was the Nazi party. But the same time, this great country accepts the Nazi party in our age. This, I think, is a terrible mistake."

The uneasiness always creeps back into their lives. Like a sixth sense, it returns at the oddest times and places. Anything can set it off. A child's face. A familiar name. A newscast. A worship service. A holiday celebration. A conversation. The critical and the casual are fraternal twins in the lives of a Holocaust survivor. So different, yet so similar. Either can remind the survivor of the pain.

Sometimes the reminder is more a warning, than a sharp, unpleasant sensation. Sometimes it is anger, or tears, or falling off an emotional cliff into the abyss of depression.

Decades in no way diminish the feelings of fear, loneliness and anger that suddenly strike. Oh, years ago, most survivors learned that there are many Americans who will never understand. Some people's knowledge of history is so limited that their under-standing of World War II begins and ends with Roosevelt and Churchill and late night reruns of daring American fighter pilots. The most astute survivors know that history looks prettier through rose-colored glasses than through the sharp binoculars of hindsight. But even those sensitive minds cannot help but feel the twinge of bitterness such callousness provokes. Pain is something survivors have lived with for so long that they can understand why others shun it. But, usually, survivors cannot fathom why any American would sit still for the perpetration of unjustice. They know that the homeland they adopted after the gruesome experiences of World War II is not perfect, but most survivors still will never accept that the United States is sometimes very naive, trusting enough to believe that the mere existence of a nation

Like all of us, survivors have heard the platitudes, even repeated them aloud sometimes. "That would never happen here." "That's all in the past." "Adolf Hitler is dead now, you're safe." "What we have to fear is nuclear war, not crimes against humanity." Repeated over and over, the statements dull the sharp stabs of fear, but they do not dispel the ever-present sense of uneasiness.

Some survivors will never tell their stories, fearing reprisal. Others tell them often, loudly, determined to ensure that no one will ever dare to intrude upon their lives again, or ever try to take away the freedom they finally found again. Others know that all of life is fleeting, security a matter of degree, not constancy. Theirs is the pain of knowing the many faces of evil, of remembering not so much the physical scars, but the psychological wounds still buried. Once opened, the wounds might fester again, undermine the success so many survivors have worked toward for so long. So some survivors never tell their children their stories, never explain why Mother has difficulty sleeping, why Father angers so easily. Instead, they continue. The throb of pain lessens over the years, sometimes becoming only a dull ache. But, for others, it lies far beneath the courageous face the survivor has presented to the world ever since he or she was freed. Only a tragic illness, a divorce, a heated argument, or something similar may uncover it.

The survivors know that no one anywhere at anytime in any place will ever totally understand them. The most insensitive soul can be moved to sympathy. But it is only other survivors who can empathize. Psychiatrists help sometimes, but usually fail to understand. Faith helps sometimes, but it is based on belief, not fact. There are always questions. Questions of why did it happen to me? And, how did it happen to us? Why did I survive when so many others perished? The questions lie deep inside the survivor's soul, always there. Their presence is like the gaping hole in the chest of a wounded soldier. All the parts of the human being remain, but the skin of security, the sheath of normality has been irrevocably shattered. The threads of a survivor's life are fragmented, frought not so much with the knots and twists of milestones, paths chosen and rejected, but more with broken pieces, final ends. These cuts aren't even frayed pieces, but abrupt breaks in the network of a life history. Breaks like a child sent to one side, the line where people died, when a parent followed orders

The Memories

(Left) Picture taken in Displaced Persons Camp in Poking, Germany, 1946.

(Bottom) Picture taken in Lodz, Poland, in Summer 1945, when Eva and Shelly were united with husband and father, Meyer.

Eva and Meyer Weiner and their daughter Shelly, survivors who were hidden by Ukrainian farmers until they were liberated by the Russian Army in February 1944.

Lt. Glenn Farthing in ROTC Uniform — Liberator, Dachau Concentration Camp.

The Romer Family: *(seated)* Mother, Henriette, died in Auschwitz; Father, Peter, survived. *(Standing, left to right)* Burt's brothers Siegfried and Roland died in Oranienburg; Burt, survivor.

Sergeant Carlton Raper *(center)* Liberator, Dachau Concentration Camp, with fellow service men at Diemeriengen in Alsace, twelve miles from German border, winter of 1944.

Susan Cernyak-Spatz, survivor. Auschwitz Concentration Camp — her identification card and permit for entry into Belgium, August 1945. Burt Romer, survivor — his German identification with "J" Stamp.

(Left to Right) Hedy Hekler Segal, Donald Hekler, Erica Hekler, Children of Ursula and Norman Hekler, survivors of Westerbörk Concentration Camp.

Nelly Falk, mother of Walter Falk, gassed at
Auschwitz.

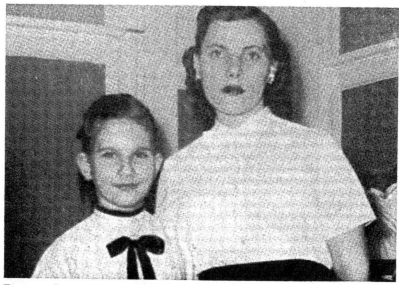

Florence Goemaat and her mother; child of survivor, born in 1948 at Bergen-
Belson Displaced Persons Camp in Germany.

Esther Mordechai, survivor, Auschwitz Concentration Camp, shown with her
family in happier days. Esther was the only survivor in this family picture.

Morris Kiel, American Army Oficer in Nurnberg, Germany, 1946; Chief,
Counter Intelligence Corps during Major War Crimes Trials.

CHAPTER 6
REACHING OUT

Gizella Abramson's gray-green eyes glow with the warmth of a balmy ocean breeze as she opens her door to me one Saturday afternoon. Crystal clear streams of spring sunlight frame her perky face and short blond hair. She is younger, livelier, than I had expected. Barely 5 feet tall, she talks non-stop as she ushers me into her living room.

Decorated in warm earth shades, the house is as welcoming as she is. There are bright Impressionist paintings. Books on Israel. Throw pillows casually tossed into the corner of a couch. Family photographs are tucked into a frame designed for picture collages in the den. A coffee pot percolates in the kitchen.

This might be the home of almost anyone in this sunny, suburban Raleigh, N.C., neighborhood. What is different is not the house, but its owner. Abramson's personal history, her devotion to Judaism and her dedication to telling others about the Nazi Holocaust are mainstays in her life. First we sip coffee, trading pleasantries and I answer questions about myself. Eventually, she reluctantly lets me turn the conversation around, to focus on her.

For several hours, she talks. She moves from the past to the present, hopping and skipping from her wartime experiences in a Jewish ghetto, to her life today, then back to the 18 months she spent as part of the Polish Resistance during World War II.

Little remains of the scarred, frightened young woman who moved to the United States after the war. But still Abramson dredges up the memories, intent on telling a story from which others can learn. A member of the North Carolina Council on the Holocaust, she began talking first at high schools, churches and civic clubs, whenever she was asked. That work began before the council came into being.

As she describes her childhood, bright Polaroid-perfect images coalesce into a silent montage of pastoral beauty.

Born Gizella Gross in Poland in a town called Tarnopol, she paints vivid pictures of her life before the war, before Adolf Hitler eradicated the only world she had ever known.

'My family was very unusual because they owned land, and not many Jews owned land. My memories are of the house, and of the soil, and of how the house smelled on Shabbat (the Jewish Sabbath). It was scrubbed clean, and I remember the smell of the Sabbath dinner. The candles were on the table. Later, when times were bad, and I felt lonely, so alone and hungry, I always thought of the lit candles, and of the family and of the Seder (the Passover Seder). And I always hoped that I would be able to experience this feeling once again."[24]

The feeling is swathed in memories of a family whose history was cut short. "I spent a lot of time with my (maternal) grandparents. I adored my grandmother, and my grandmother and I were soulmates. Actually, to a great extent, I owe my life to my grandmother." Her grandmother, Rachel Schecter, groomed her, taught her, coaching her in some of the very skills she later used to survive.

Rachel Schecter was born near the German-Austrian border. Abramson cannot remember in which country.

"She spoke fluent German. She taught me Goethe. Kotzebue and Schiller. I had to memorize their poetry. ... My grandmother said to me when I was 5 years old, 'One of these days, you will inherit this land, and I am going to teach you you what you will have to do.' She said, 'In order for the people to do a good job for you, you have to know how to do it yourself.'

"My grandmother took me to the barn. We had milkmaids because Poland did not have milking machines. My grandmother asked one of the milkmaids to stand up. Then, she, whom I had never seen do menial work, sat on the milking stool and showed me how to milk the cow."

About a decade later, Gizella Abramson remembered that lesson, and many, many others. The tale of how those memories shaped her life begins in 1939, the first time she remembers talk of war invading the security of her childhood world. Her father, Marcel Gross, was in the Polish army reserves.

In '39, war broke out. By September, Poland was partitioned between Nazi Germany and Russia, while Lithuania annexed the Vilna region.[25] Russia occupied the part of Poland where Abramson and her family lived. With that occupation came the first change. The Abramson family was forced to leave their farm for an apartment in Przemysl. They lived in one room. Refugees lived in other rooms. Kitchen and bathroom facilities had to be shared. Soon, Jewish children were separated from other youngsters, sent to an all-Jewish school. Then, bit by bit, Abramson noticed that her school mates and their families began to disappear. One day, her friends came to school, the next day they did not.

"I don't remember how many friends disappeared. I kept asking, 'What happened to them? The whole family disappeared.' "

Her parents evaded the questions, sticking to their belief that children should be sheltered from the fear and turmoil swirling through Poland. But a time came when Hannah and Marcel Gross knew they had to face the truth themselves, and prepare their children, Gizella, and her only sibling, Zenon, a younger brother. The people who disappeared were sent to Siberia, the children were told.

Soon she went to stay with her Aunt Lucy and Uncle Janek in Lutsk. Her parents believed she would be safer. Her only communication with her immediate family soon was an occasional clandestine letter. By then, Germans controlled that part of Poland, and Jews were trying only to survive. Soon Gizella and her aunt and uncle were herded into a Jewish ghetto, sequestered away from the rest of the community. Their property—including jewelry, most clothing and household furnishings—was confis-

There was only one water pump, and it was padlocked except for one hour a day. There was no food, no sanitation. There was typhoid and starvation everywhere.

'They brought Jews from all over. Imagine the population of Durham, Chapel Hill and Raleigh crammed into an area the size of the N.C. State University campus.

'There were random killings every day. One day I watched a work detail coming back into the ghetto. All at once the Germans started shooting for no reason and cut half of them down.

'Each day trucks came and took people away, and every day the line at the water pump was smaller and smaller. You could hear the sound of screaming and moaning every night. The Germans said they were relocating people to safety where they could work with honor, a Jewish committee was forced to select who was to go. They forced the deported people to write postcards back to the ghetto so that people would not panic.' ''

Her Uncle Janek, a skilled physician loved by his patients, had more freedom of movement than many who lived in the ghetto.[27] With him, Abramson's double life began. In the ghetto, she was a Jew. Outside, with her blonde hair and gray-green eyes, she might be mistaken for a German or a Pole. Whenever her uncle might be summoned by Christian patients beyond the ghetto's walls, his niece might go with him, carrying his medical bag. When she could, she also slipped out at other times. Sometimes Jewish children risked all, sneaking beyond the ghetto's wall and then trying to sell a piece of clothing or other valuable smuggled in much earlier. Whatever they could sell or trade went for food.

One day Uncle Janek sent for Abramson, asking her to bring a special implement to the home of a Czech farmer he was treating.

"I walked out without my yellow patches ... And suddenly I hear, 'Eh, Kleines? Wohin gehst Du? Wohin gehst Du, Kleines?' Where are you going, little one? I was walking with my head bowed. They were German soldiers calling me, 'Now look at her,' they said. 'How pretty. She looks like my — look at the blonde hair. Look at those eyes. Do you want a piece of chocolate?'

"I remember walking on. I didn't turn around then ... I came to the farm, and I must have looked a bit strange. Uncle says to me, 'What's the matter with you? You look positively yellow. And where are your patches?' ''

Uncle Janek turned to the wife of the farmer he was treating. "Do me a favor," he said, "put the patches on her." But the farmer's wife shook her head. "She looked at me," Abramson recalls, "and she said, 'No, I won't. She doesn't need any patches. She doesn't look Jewish.' "

Her words were prophetic. Abramson's supervisors told her the same thing once she went to work with the Polish Resistence. But, in spite of her looks, life was no easy matter in the ghetto for Abramson. More Jews died, or were sent away. Uncle Janek soon decided to take the suggestion of a Czech farmer who was his patient and hide his wife and children in the loft of a friendly farmer's barn. (Abramson's uncle did not survive the war, but her Aunt Lucy and two of her cousins, Emiel and Genie, did. Thanks goes to the Czech farmers who hid them.) Soon it was decided that Abramson too must find a safe haven and go to stay with another of her uncle's patients.

"We were to meet at a meadow on the edge of town," she remembers.[28] "I heard trucks coming and hid. When they arrived, they were full of people. The Germans yelled at them to get down, and I saw a shower of yellow stars as they got off. They made the people dig trenches as they argued about how deep the trenches should be. Then they lined everyone up by the trench and made them disrobe.

"There was a command to fire, and they started shooting. I saw one lady holding her baby. She was smiling and kissing her baby with tears streaming down as the bullets hit her. There was screaming for a while, and then it got quiet. Those voices have haunted me every day of my life.

"The Germans left, and I crept out. Blood was rising to the top of that pit. I was standing and looking at it when two men grabbed me."

As she was grabbed, she turned and said, "What do you want?[29] And then somebody put his hands on me, and I was placed under straw in the wagon. They said, 'You be quiet. ... Look, we know who your aunt is. We know who you are.'

"And that was the beginning. I was taken to a peasant home.

Veronika. ... The birth certificate was authentic, but the only problem was Veronika was much older than I. So the next picture that you might see of me, I had put my hair up so that I looked a little bit older. I remember thinking that I looked much more mature."

Two men captured her the day she saw the Germans slaughter the Jews. One of her captors went with her as a witness when she sought identification papers — required for everyone under Nazi rule in that region. Beforehand, her captor/witness coached her, brutally drumming her new identity into her head.

"He spoke Polish to me. He spoke fluent Russian. He would correct my Russian. He would correct my Ukrainian, never my Polish. My German was better than his. He said, 'I want you to tell them that you live in a village.' That village was where my birth certificate said I was from. He told me, 'Say you have a sore throat and that you have come to be cured in Lutsk. You have a sore throat.'

"At night, he would shine a light in my face to wake me up. He would say, 'What's your name?' 'Gizella Gross.' 'What's your name?' SLAP. 'Veronika?' 'WHAT'S YOUR NAME?' 'VERONIKA!' "

Abramson, barely a teenager at the time, quickly learned the essential lesson. "That way I became conditioned. When I went for that certificate, I was Veronika." After obtaining the identification papers, she began her work with the Resistance. At her first job, she was told that she would know only one person among her comrades. "The person that I was to know was named Makar. ... Throughout my stay, I only knew that one man. I was so naive that I didn't even ask why until I was sent on my second job, and I was given a different identity. I never was permitted to ask any questions. Nothing. If I did, their standard answer was: 'None of your business. None of your business.'

"At that first job, I was supposed to be a granddaughter and a niece in this house, which was a nicer home than most in that neighborhood. The commandant, the German commandant in that city, lived in that house. My job was to polish his boots, bring his meals, empty the wastepaper basket."

Also living in the house were a Polish man and an older woman who pretended to be Abramson's uncle and grandmother.

61

"Anything I found in the wastepaper basket, I was told to bring it to Makar. My job was to live in this house. ... Never ask any questions ... And tell Makar about the comings and goings of the German officers, and the types of insignia they were wearing. And I was to listen to what was said."

She was told: "Pretend you do not understand German so that you can listen to their conversation. Be like a kitten. Ingratiate yourself."

Sometimes, when she supposedly went out on a household errand, she sneaked off to meet Makar. At all times, she stayed alert to conversations   and to the commandant's trash can. When no one was looking, she would retrieve bits and pieces of paper from the trash can, stuff them in her bodice, and later turn them over to Makar.

"I was always, always, on guard. It was ridiculous. I had no choice of where to go, what to do. They knew my real name. They knew where my parents were. I think my parents were in Przemysl. They knew where my aunt and cousins were. They had me right in their hands. ... They said they would help my family."

With her loved ones in mind, she gradually adapted to her role. Her life of deception became easier and easier. Believing that her aunt and cousins would be killed if she did not do as she was told, she kept working for the Resistance, burying her memories of her past, praying her brother and her parents were safe. She learned to meet Makar at the farmers' market and to pass information to him as she bought vegetables and fruits

"You would be surprised how easy it was when you thought of it. You were able to figure out how to do these things. You do not always have to be taught. Maybe they knew that I had this ability, and that I could, intuitively, find ways. Maybe that was my skill—that and those languages that I knew."

Almost as abruptly as she arrived at the German commandant's house, Abramson left, departing under the wing of the woman who was supposed to be her grandmother.

"I was the cleaning person. This was where my real grandmother's teaching came in. She had taught me how to clean and wash clothes. I could scrub a floor. In Poland, the floors were made of wood, but they were not polished floors. They were planks."

Her assignment was to steal as many copies of the identification and provision forms as she could. "People could survive with those papers. ... I never knew who they gave them to. That's what I wonder about today. I would like to know that I saved someone's life. Maybe they saved some Jews."

Again, there was one person to whom she reported. His name was Tadek. A younger man than Makar, he was all business. "He said, 'You will be a link in the chain.' That's what I was — a link in the chain."

At her next job, she was still in Lutsk, in a house quite near the home of the old man where she had worked before. The home had belonged to a Jew. "Here I had to cook, clean, do the laundry."

By then, it was about 1943. Abramson recalls a lot about her first identity. But the others blur together. Barely a teenager when her work with the Resistance began, she grew up quickly. What she does remember from this period are the basic facts. She always had a different name. She usually pretended to be someone older than herself. She was always an orphan. Early in 1944, she was captured.

"I think somebody denounced me," she said. "I don't know for sure."

At the time, she was working with a German supply unit, doing kitchen work. A Gestapo officer came. He asked many questions. Even though the Germans could not prove her identity was false, because she had the proper identification papers, Abramson was arrested.

Where was she taken? What happened next?

She shrugs off the questions.

"I was in and out of concentration camps," she says. "That's a concentration-camp existence. Those stories are known. It's like anybody else's."

World War II ended in 1945. Both Abramson's parents and her younger brother were dead. She emigrated to the United States to live with an aunt and uncle in New York. A smoldering hate burned inside her.

"Nothing made me happy. I remember I was like a machine. I ate. I answered questions. But I was dead inside. Why? Why? Why? A person's profile would remind me of someone I knew who was killed. ... When my aunt made a rare roast beef, the sight of blood made me ill to my stomach. I ran to the bathroom. One day she made hamburgers. The smell of the charred meat brought back the smell of the oven. And I hated. I hated so.

"They lived in Brooklyn. One day I was taking a walk, I heard two women speaking German. I turned around. There must have been such hatred on my face. These women looked and ran away.

"And I realized that I was given a chance and that it was up to me to do something with my life. I could not hold onto this hate. I felt that the hate would eat me up, and whatever God-given ability I had, I would not be able to use. I realized that, 'I must not let Hitler win. He will not kill me.' If I did not change, I knew sooner or later — I would break down. That's how I started. I would take one step forward, and two steps backwards. But I knew that, if God, in his mercy and wisdom, let me live, I had to do something productive with my life.

"I am his partner. This was the beginning."

She went on to graduate from college, and meet and marry her husband, Paul, now an engineer with IBM. They moved to North Carolina. They have two grown children, Michael and Holly.

Abramson's time is devoted to her family, her work with the Holocaust Council, and her job as religious education director for Temple Beth Or in Raleigh. She is passionate about most subjects, but most passionate when she talks about her faith and her love for the United States.

"I want to prevent atrocities like that from ever happening again," she says. "People have to believe that it happened to the Jews and it can happen again. People must believe that every human being has a right to believe in their own God in their own

Oh, I used to get angry with God. But, in the long run, what happened is a part of Him that I don't understand. It happened. It's much easier to believe than not to believe.

"It seems to me that what pulled me through, what helped me not to become a thief, a murderer. ... was this faith and the Golden Rule. ... I don't know if you have this feeling talking to other survivors, that our life is a miracle. We don't know why we survived."

CHAPTER 7
STARTING OVER

More than 30 years after Bramy Resnik came to the United States, an Old World charm still flavors his manners and demeanor. He is courteous and solicitous when I arrive at his home in Greenville, N.C.

"Did you have a comfortable trip? Did it take too long to get here?" he asks.[32] "Oh, yes, the tape recorder. Put it here on the coffee table. No, don't worry, it won't hurt anything. Can I take your jacket? Your purse? Do you need an extension cord? No? Well, would you like a cup of coffee?"

The gracious overtures continue until Resnik leaves briefly to fix the coffee. I sit down, my fingers roving through the tape recorder carrying case for the two pancake microphones. "The coffee will be ready soon," he announces upon his return.

"I didn't want to do this," he confides. "I was going to tell you, 'No.' But then I thought about it and decided you should come."

Four hours later, after an interview that tracks through the feelings of a small boy to the bitterness of a young man finally released from a Nazi labor camp, I find out why Resnik said yes.

"There were two reasons," he says. "One is that my good friend, Rabbi (Arnold S.) Task, said, 'Bramy, you're not doing your job.' And what is my job? That's the important thing. And I must agree born — let's say they were 5-year-olds, slightest memory they could have (of the Holocaust). Right? From 1940, they are now — What? 45 years old ... So they're going to be dying out.

"You see, I'm past 55. As my kids say, I'm over the hill. So the story has to be told, as painful as it may be. And it is — I must tell you. It is painful. I think it has to be told. The world has to know, whether it is via tape or via written paper, it has to be told. People have to know whether they're Jews or non-Jews.

"The echoes that one hears that it was a lie, that it didn't exist. I cannot stand by and let someone say that. Recently there was advertising in one of the most prestigious German-American journals called *The German Quarterly*. A gentleman who claims to be a historian, a former German professor, retired, is part of a revisionist school. He has published a book that denies the existence of the Holocaust.

"When this happens, I cannot stand by and say, 'You mean I suffered all these years for you to say that I didn't suffer? You mean it was an aberration of my mind? It was a dream? I wish it were a dream."

Before the nightmare, Resnik lived on a peaceful farm in the countryside outside Prague, Czechoslovakia. Born Abraham Resnik (later shortened to just 'Bramy'), he was the only son of Berta Wasserman and Herman Resnik. His mother was Czech, his father Russian. He had one older sister, Sylvia. She died in Israel, where she had immigrated after living briefly in the United States following the Holocaust.

"My father was what is known here in the United States as a gentleman farmer. We had a large piece of land on the outskirts of Prague and a fairly decent house ... Within that area, we were the first to have central heating, bathrooms. ... My father was a representative for a Czech firm and he traveled extensively. He traveled extensively through Europe. Sometimes he would have to be a year in an area and we would go with him, so to speak, resettle with him in an area."

Resnik remembers snatches of that time, brief glimpses of the peace and pleasure of his early childhood. "It was a very warm situation," he says. "I remember distinctly we had a tremendously large cellar where we used to keep our food for the winter, because winters are quite severe in that area. ... It is a beautiful memory because, in the winter, we would play around there. I remember Mama and Papa — just before winter would start — people would come. And we'd buy all kinds of plums and potatoes and flowers and fruits, and vegetables that could be stored. Apples and pears, for example, could be stored in the cellar. They would actually keep for a long period of time.

"But I remember just before the weather would turn very, very cold, when harvest time came, we would have a tremendous amount of cooking going on, preserving all kinds of jams and making all kinds of things in bottles. Here you would make ketchup. We would make all kinds of sauces and all kinds of things that were put in bottles and then preserved in the basement."

"We would also buy wine, by the kegs, which was used for partying or for other purposes. ... And we would play in the basement. Neighbors and friends would come over, non-Jews, by the way. We were the only Jews living in that area, only Jewish family. But there were non-Jews, very good friends ... We had religious observances. But we were in a sense what you would call assimilated Jews. We are more religious, I think, now in North Carolina than we were ever religious in Europe, that is, in Czechoslovakia."

"I was approaching my teens when the war started," Resnik recalls. "Before the Germans took over Czechoslovakia in 1939, he says, "My parents were aware of the fact that they were coming. Nothing could be helped. I know I remember distinctly that many of our non-Jewish friends who were military took off and went to Poland. In fact, some of them were taken by the Russians. Poland was subdivided, that is, divided between the Germans and the Russians. And many of them (his family's friends) were in Siberia. ... Jews usually have relatives all over. And we had relatives in Poland; we had relatives in France, in Belgium. Of all my relatives, a big clan, I would say, there are very few left. You could

"And, I recall distinctly discussing how Hitler would never do it. (They would say,) 'It's impossible, just a threat.' So a few Jews would suffer, but the rest, he wouldn't dare do anything to them."

Looking back, Resnik is certain that no one in his family believed the Third Reich and its fanatical leader possibly could muster the power and support to dominate most of Europe. A few months after the Germans marched into Czechoslovakia, the unbelievable came true.

What happened when the Germans came?

Resnik knits his long fingers together, lights another Virginia Slims menthol cigarette. He takes a long drag on the cigarette. As he answers, the smoke he has inhaled comes out of this mouth in short puffs, punctuating his story.

"In fact, the basement served as a hiding place for us for a very short period of time," he says.

The Germans had imposed a curfew on local citizenry which the elderly couple, who were caretakers of the Resniks' farm, violated.

"They left the house before a curfew and were shot. And we (his family) got out of that basement and looked for them. We saw them on the street; and we were caught, but not shot because it was daytime," Resnik says.

His memory of the details blurs, but he recalls, "We were hiding for quite a while at a neighbor's house after we walked out of our house.

"And then, we were caught and taken to a holding place. ... And one of the officers happened to have been a neighbor of my parents when were were living in Berlin, prior to Hitler. He recognized mother; and all I remember is that she said, 'Hans?' and he said, 'Berta.' And what has transpired is that Mother bought us out with some of the jewelry that we had."

After being released from that holding place, which Resnik thinks was actually Theresienstadt, a camp 40 miles from Prague, the family went to Poland.

"It was in the — just across the border. I've forgotten the name of it. ... It's a little Jewish town, quite a few Jews there. In fact, one relative of my father, cousin of father, lived there."

The Resniks made their way to the little town by using fake passports identifying them as foreigners, citizens of countries not then at war with Germany. Because they had the passports, they were allowed to cross the border into Poland.

They remained in Poland for a few months, Resnik says, until they heard that the Germans were moving into that section. At the time, the Germans and the Russians made an agreement to divide Poland. The Resniks fled from the region where they had been living, now controlled by Germany, to the other side of Poland, under Russian control. Their flight proved futile, however.

The minute they crossed the border they were placed in a Russian prison because of the fake passports they were carrying. Resnik remembers that the prison was a jail of sorts where prisoners were allowed blankets and mattresses and were given decent food. But all their valuables, jewelry and personal clothing were confiscated. The Resniks' car also was taken.

"My father spoke a little bit of Russian, of course, My mother spoke Czech. ... And we always wanted to talk to someone in charge. We could never talk to someone in charge. Finally one day there was this gentleman who we could tell — this officer — that he was in charge. The way he walked around and the guards walking after him.

"He was a Russian colonial who happened to be Jewish. Not only that, but he came from the same area that my father and his parents came from. And, in fact, he remembered my grandparents and took us out (of jail). And we had a big party at his house, introduced us to his wife, who was also Jewish. He, in fact, arranged the papers (documents needed to be released). ... He got hold of a car for us and found an apartment for us. He arranged it in such a way that we were not prisoners anymore. ... We became Russian citizens, so to speak, almost. We were now legally in the occupied area."

It was 1940 or 1941. Resnik cannot remember the exact year. To support the family, Resnik's father got a job as a watchman. The family had food again. Resnik and his sister attended school. He took a normal load of academic studies at a predominantly Jewish school, and his sister was training at a trade school. Life was almost normal for 6 to 8 months. Then the family's Russian friend, the colonel, alerted them one day that the Germans were advancing. The colonel's name was Joseph.

"One day," Resnik says, "I remember Joseph called us up and said, 'We are leaving. Leave with us. The Germans are coming. We know the Germans are not too keen on the Jews.' And my papa came home, I remember, and said, 'Pack.' So there wasn't much to pack up anyway. And we packed up. And I remember all I had was one pair of shoes. ... So we got into the car that was given to us by Joseph, filled it up with gas; and we had a few more gallons of gas that we put in the trunk. And we took off with the Russian army that was retreating into Russia. ... We just started following the Russian army that was pulling out of the Ukraine. ... We went all the way, almost, to Kiev, in the Ukraine, almost a little village or town. That's where the car broke down and we couldn't go any further. And the Russians were just running back and forth.

"And then the parachutes came down — German parachutes — and we were caught. ... We didn't have any documents. The only thing we had — a statement from Joseph's paper that we were Czechs. And, based on that, we tried to tell them we were German, because all of us spoke German, that we were Germans who were taken prisoner by the Russians. They bought it for about a week. And then, after, they said, 'No, you are not. You are Jews.' And we were immediately put in a truck with other Jews that they rounded up and were taken to a holding area where we heard a lot of shooting going on. There were thousands of people there. Thousands. They were shooting Jews. They were shooting fifty at a time, all at one time. They put them in a ditch, shot them, the ditch filled up, they called a group, in columns. We were in line to be shot, the rest of us. And somehow, I don't know. They stopped the shooting after a few days. And we were placed in a truck and taken to an area.

"This was a big, former Russian military base. And there were lots of barracks. And we were placed in the barracks, crammed 300 or 400 in a barracks that would house only about, maybe 50.

"And we were stripped of clothes, walked around naked. Our hairs were shorn, even the pubic area. And I didn't have hair, not that much that you could think of. ... This was funny. ... They didn't have electric clippers, hand clippers (only). They came up to me and said, 'You don't have much. GO.'

"So, it was the first time that I saw my mother and my sister and my father naked. I've seen my father naked before. It was the first

71

time I saw thousands of people naked. We were given striped uniforms — "

His voice trails off. Resnik, a meticulously proper, private man, carefully removes his glasses. With one finger, he wipes a tear from his right eye. "Sorry," he says, quietly, and begins anew.

"And, then, we were separated into women and men. While standing in line, we were asked what kind of jobs we did. And the words, well the line, (came into my mind): 'Say you're a tailor. Say you're a tailor.' And, I stood on my toes to look big and said: 'I'm a tailor.' And we were placed in a tailor shop ... my father, and also a cousin of ours who we met on the way. And, it seems, that both my mother and my sister were also in the tailor shop "

Resnik was told he was in Mogilev, a camp where death came "by attrition, starvation." The only way to survive was to work.

"My father lost an arm because he tried to escape, believing a rumor that we were going to be shot. His arm was literally severed off with a submachine gun. Severed off. ... He was close to a guard who emptied the magazine of his gun into him. But, somehow, it missed most of the body here." Resnik points to his chest. "Which was very close to the heart. But, somehow, it just bypassed the heart. But it severed his arm off.

"Somehow he was brought with us because the Germans didn't like to lose prisoners. If they did, they wanted to know they were dead. He was brought (I think) because my mother was working as a nurse. This place actually was not just a labor camp. It was a transition hospital for German soldiers on the way back to the front.

"We were placed on a farm, for example, for two or three months to work on a farm. ... They needed some laborers in some factory, and we had to go there. We'd clean up, or move heavy equipment, or clean the railroad tracks, or work on all kinds of things, depending on what they felt like. And you just went. ... You either walked — if it wasn't too far, or you went on a truck. They placed you in a truck. If you tried to escape, of course, if they caught you, they'd shoot you."

Life was a treadmill. Prisoners got up at 4 a.m.; waited in lines

lines. "And there was no hot coffee, no hot tea," Resnik adds ironically. "And we went to work."

They worked in freezing temperatures. "We had a routine. Each one would take turns sleeping for 10 to 15 minutes on someone else's shoulder. It wasn't a big camp, just a few thousand. ... And every day, groups would be assigned to different work outside the camp.

"It wasn't a pleasant life. ... In the beginning, I remember, everything was congenial, and we tried to help each other. But in a very short time, everyone became, I would say, selfish for 'Numero Uno.' "

Resnik was in a different camp from his mother and sister, a different barracks from his father. His father's chief fear was that his son would be killed because rumors kept circulating that young people were not needed for the camp work detail. Bramy Resnik never was taken away, however. He missed the death his father feared: being drowned in a nearby lake where the Nazis disposed of a group of 5- and 6-year-old children.

"I could work for hours and never get, well, not get tired, but not show tiredness. I was tired, exhausted. Lack of food. We would get one piece of bread — size of a pack of cigarettes — a day. And then, we had a can. Each one had a can, but no spoon. We were not allowed the luxury of a spoon. ... We were given some kind of soup, it was called. If you looked, things were floating around in the soup that were alive, supposedly. ... The German guard would watch, and if you didn't want to eat it. ... And they would actually urinate into the can and tell you to drink. If you didn't, they would shoot you."

"And you learned to eat that shit. Excuse me. That junk. And you were glad you had something to eat. ... And one of the greatest fears, I remember, was not to become, you know, to show any discharge of blood. Discharge of blood meant instantaneous death. ... It meant you were shot because you were gone. The minute you started discharging blood, you were out. Dysentery. ... You learned how to bear the cold, freezing, turning blue. You learned how to live with it, rubbing yourself as best you could to stay alive.

"You always thought of yourself. You didn't think about the suffering of others. In a normal situation, when you see someone suffering, you feel pity, compassion. You didn't have any more compassion or feelings. So Papa said he didn't feel well. So what? He didn't feel well. I didn't feel well either. So what help could I be to him? I'm sure he felt the same way, although I was his flesh and blood."

One way Resnik survived was becoming the servant of a German officer. "In fact, I became his 'boot boy'. ... He would boot me in the ass, as well as I would clean his boots and clean his uniform and iron his uniform. ... And when he would turn around, I would steal from his locker. ... Eventually I sewed myself secret pockets into my uniform. ... And whenever I was on a farm, I would put food into the secret pockets. They were baggy anyway and nobody could see it. And eventually I would bring my father and my father's cousin — I would bring food."

After ingratiating himself with the German, Resnik also became "part-time helper, slave," to another soldier, an officer who liked him because he spoke French and German and knew a little about literature.

"He, at one time, gave me food. I couldn't believe it. He gave me half a salami. Or he would send me to get milk, and I would spill a little bit and then get on the floor and lick. And he took great joy to see me lick on the floor. He wouldn't give me a cup of milk."

Food was food. It meant survival, Resnik says. "It didn't matter where it came from, if it came from the garbage. My children today laugh at me. I'm a garbage man, they say. I still cannot see food thrown out. It hurts me. It hurts me to see food thrown out."

Resnik also was befriended by a German nurse, who was a Jehovah's Witness. The nurse was forced to work for the Nazis after they put her parents in a concentration camp. "She took me under wing. About four months, I was her cleaning boy, her pet, if you want to. She gave me food, enough food that I could get for my father and cousin. Smuggle, of course, nobody could know, because if the other inmates would know, they would rip me apart, knowing that I had food. We would sneak it and hold in the hand little pieces, so nobody would know

"We didn't share it with other people.   As my stomach became full, I realized that I have a father. I have relatives in the camp. I would try to go next to the fence and try to give food to my sister."

For 4½ years, Resnik lived, on and off, in Mogilev. Sometimes he and other laborers were taken away to Bergen-Belsen, a horrible death and labor camp, to work. "Wherever they needed laborers, they took us."

In 1944, he escaped "and became a partisan. The rumor was that the Russians were advancing. ... We only found out after the war. In fact, only found out here when I was in the United States, that one of the reasons many of us escaped, or some of them rebelled at the last minute, was they found out the Germans were afraid to leave anyone alive to tell what has happened.

When he escaped, Resnik still was working for a German lieutenant, one of the officers he had worked for all along. He would give Resnik special permission to leave the camp to go out and buy things for him. Because he still wore a camp inmate's uniform, Resnik did not try to escape for a long time. But one day, he had a brief chance to talk to his mother, who said, "If you have a chance, escape. I heard rumors that people are being — are going to be killed."

So, Resnik took off. "I had a pass, and rather than come back, I kept going until I reached the wood. In the woods, I found some other people hiding there. And I wanted food and they said, 'Sure, there is food.' And they gave me some food, some raw potatoes, some carrots, and radishes. ... And I ate. And I said, 'Where do you buy this?' Very foolishly. And they said, 'No, we don't buy it. I'll show you how you, too, can get it, because we don't have much for you. You'll have to get your own food.'

The partisans numbered 10 to 15 people. Each carried some sort of gun, usually one stolen from a German soldier. Resnik got a gun, after killing, with a knife, a soldier who stood guard at a railroad overpass near the partisans' hideout.

"And I got the boots and I got the coat. And I had finally some warm clothes for the first time in years. It was unfortunate to kill someone. It's not a pleasure. It's something you live with the rest of your life. You can see the picture of that person before your eyes every time you talk about it or think about it, or try to fall asleep. It always comes back. It was another human being. He was not part of the concentration camp. He was given the duty. But I'm sure that he would have shot me if he had seen the knife."

Resnik lived with the partisans in the woods for several months until the Russians advanced into the area of Mogilev. Like thousands of other civilians and military, his small group followed the Russian soldiers, to liberate Mogilev. When the war ended, Resnik and his family eventually ended up in a displaced persons camp outside the city of Wolfrathauseen. In June 1951, Resnik emigrated from Germany to the United States. His parents had emigrated a year earlier.

"Right after the war, I could hardly read or write. ... But I have always wanted an education. And I had excellent friends after the war. And some of them were Germans, German young people about my age who helped me master reading and writing."

What he did not learn through his friends, he taught himself, reading chemistry, philosophy, sociology, history and math texts. But he still felt he needed more education after arriving in the United States. Taking a friend's advice, Resnik enlisted in the military, mainly for the financial advantages then provided through the GI Bill. Because his father had lost an arm during the war and his mother was not working at the time, Resnik was stationed in the United States throughout his two-year tour of duty from 1955 through 1957. Although he actually had received formal schooling only through the third grade. Resnik's years of personal study served him well. He took a graduate equivalency examination while he was in the service and earned his high school diploma.

When he was discharged, he enrolled in Hunter College in New York City, where he and his parents lived. In 3½ years, he earned a degree, double-majoring in German and pre-med. His attempts to go to medical school were unsuccessful, because of his age and lack of money, so he went back to college and took education courses to be qualified to teach German at the high school level. Soon he met his wife, Rhea Ruth Schwartz, at a conference for foreign-language instructors. In a month, they were engaged, six months later they married.

'You know who you're marrying. You're marrying a European and a survivor of a concentration camp.' "

Yet Resnik's background never impeded his education. He went on to earn his master's and his doctorate in German, taught at the University of Southern California in Los Angeles (where he earned his doctorate) and moved to North Carolina in the fall of 1968, after getting a job on the faculty of East Carolina University.

"When we came to Greenville, Greenville was known to my wife and I as a 'one-horse town.' It was an extremely small town except for the student body that has always been large. ... In my view, I liked the smallness at the time better than I like it now because bigness brings the problems of a metropolitan area — crime increases, prostitution, drugs, traffic. ... But at the same time, it brings prosperity, it brings healthy competition, and perhaps a better need for better education. So you do have — with evil, you have the good."

"I was looking for a job close to New York. I had the opportunity to go in New York, but we had become accustomed to warm weather."

Resnik was living in California when the job teaching German at East Carolina came open. He still teaches there and the mild climate that drew him to eastern North Carolina still pleases him. High on his list also are the city's people and the life he has been able to provide his daughter, Colette, and his son, Howard.

"I still have to muse at the statement that, 'Ya'll come and visit us' when you see someone," Resnik says with a smile. "Of course, they don't literally mean it, but it's very nice."

For 17 years, Resnik kept his past a closed book, only revealing it after being asked to speak at a local high school by a student he knew from his involvement in a Greenville synagogue.

"I try to suppress many of the things. I don't want to — This is why I don't want anyone here. ... I don't think I would go to psychiatric treatment to talk about it. What's going to help me?"

Like many survivors, Resnik says, he made the transition to life in the United States by leaning on other survivors. "We helped each other, crying on each other's shoulder, but didn't talk about our experience. It became a personal property. It became something that — we just didn't talk about it. As two people who have had sex with each other   they don't go around talking about it. Right?"

"This analogy is perfect, because you don t go around talking.

We didn't go around talking. 'Gee, I was over there and you were over there. What did you do? What did you suffer?' No it's something you try to keep to yourself."

CHAPTER 8
ALWAYS AN OUTSIDER

We are sitting in the comfortable living room, decorated in white, green and gold, of Esther and Elias Mordechai's home on Madison Avenue in Greensboro, N.C. This is Esther's interview, and she is visibly nervous at the prospect of talking about her experiences during World War II. Elias, a voluble fellow, sits beside me at the table during the interview. He kneads his fingers of one hand into the palm of another, struggling to be quiet as Esther slowly, carefully answers questions.

With a little prodding, she does well. Her tale is sad in the telling, but seems to have a happy ending until we start talking about her transition from the safe shelter of her hometown, Jannina, Greece, to Auschwitz in 1944, to Jannina again in 1945, to Athens in 1950 and to America in 1951.

"We left Greece in 1951, September 15, 1951. Yesterday was exactly 33 years since we left Greece," Esther Mordechai says. (It is September 16, 1984) "We stay four days in New York. October 4, 1951, we come to Greensboro."[33]

With them, Elias and Esther Mordechai brought their two tiny daughters, Evelyn, a preschooler, and Annie, a toddler. Esther's great-uncle and uncle lived in Greensboro.

"So we came to Greensboro. And we rent one room and a kitchen on Spring Street. And we had to divide the bathroom with four other families. ... We stayed in that small apartment 27 days. We didn't even make it a month."

They moved to a bigger place for 18 months, then bought a home on Spring Street, moving in on April 4, 1953. But two years after her arrival, Esther Mordechai still felt uncomfortable in her adopted city.

'I hate to tell you this. I didn't like Greensboro at all. I didn't speak the language. ... And I felt like I was lost."

"I used to walk that Spring Garden Street. That street was a place to keep my tears. It would be an ocean. I used to cry — I used to take the two kids by the hand — they was walking — and I used to walk; I cried all the way, coming and going. And for two years, he (Elias) used to come home at night. And, at the supper table, I used to cry. For two years, I said, 'Let's go back (to Greece). I don't like it up here.' "

What was hard was being the stranger, the person who was different.

"I tell you, the first five years, it was hectic, very hectic. Then the first daughter started going to school and the other one went to school, you know, soon. And I told my husband — this is really something — I told my husband I was desperate to get out of the house. I see the other ladies working. I says, 'I'm able to sew.' I says, 'I'm going to find me a job. As soon as I put the second daughter in the first grade, I'm going to go get me a job.' "

He says, 'You think you can find a job?' And I says, 'You don't speak the language. How did anybody hire you?' I said, 'I'm going to try.'

So she took her youngest daughter to school one morning and struck out towards a local department store. "I went up there. And I went straight upstairs in the office. And the only thing I can say, I say, 'I'm a seamstress, I know how to sew.'

Those few words were enough. It was the time of year, Mordechai remembers, when women whose fingers were nimble with a needle were in demand to do alterations at the department store. They told her, "You come tomorrow and start working, and we're going to start paying you 70 cents an hour." She started the next day and worked part-time at the store, Thalhimer's, for 21 years. After a brief time at home during which she again was bored, and eager for work, she got another job. This time she was a seamstress at Brownhill's department store at Friendly Shopping Center in Greensboro. She made friends, became active in the local Reform Jewish temple and reared her two daughters. But somewhere deep down inside, the edginess of the woman who cried and paced the sidewalks of Spring Garden Street remained.

"I'd better say this," she says. "I know the feeling from me coming from different country for as long as I live. I still going to be — you know, I'm not an American.

"I don't feel like it, because, you know, people was born here and they're different. I try to follow, you know, everything to be like the other people. But it still is something in between. I'm not there, you know, I'll never be there."

Does it have something to do with being Jewish? Is it anti-Semitism?

"No. No," she says impatiently. It has more to do with, she explains, with being from another country.

'You know, foreigners that come from a different country. It's still something inside. And I talked to some other friends; and they feel the same way. They says, 'Whatever we do, we're never going to be like Americans.' You know, it's something — We come from a different country.

"But we'll do our best. You know, what are you going to do? I try to be nice to people. I try, you know, not to hurt nobody's feelings. And I have a few — a lot of friends. And I had more friends when I was working. But, it's still — It is something inside. You're a little different than anybody else."

She is not alone in this feeling of always being different, of being forced to leave behind a homeland that was familiar, peaceful, a place where her family had lived for generations. When World War II ended, many Jews felt thay could no longer remain in their native land. Many suffered out the several years immediately following the war in displaced person camps, waiting and waiting for a chance to emigrate to Israel, the United States or elsewhere. Communism, anti-Semitism and disgust with fellow countrymen who had bowed to the Nazis forced the Jews and other persecuted minorities out.

Such a man was Tuviah Friedman, later known as a hunter of Nazi criminals. In 1946, Friedman left Poland, climbing down a mountain with a group of people and crossing the Polish border into Czechoslovakia.[34]

His feelings at the departure are recorded by Milton Meltzer in the book, *Never to Forget, The Jews of the Holocaust.* When he left, Friedman thought: "I looked behind me, at Poland. My father, his father, were buried there. Jews had lived in Poland for a thousand years, their condition fluctuating like the fever of a malaria patient. One hour back, I thought, is the country in which I was born, to which I had shown allegiance, which I had tried to love; now, here, with a packful of clothing, happy that I had succeeded in crossing its frontier, I sat catching my breath, gathering up my strength for an unknown future. I had perhaps a total of $10, and some socks and shirts and underclothing."

"Everything else is in my heart."

For many survivors, that is where memories stay, locked away from well-meaning friends, publicity promoters and even their own families. Especially during their early years in the United States, some never discussed their experiences during the Holocaust for fear of being made to feel more different than they already felt.

Almost four decades after leaving Czechoslovakia, Bramy Resnik still remembers how it was.

"I'm not afraid. I was ashamed,"[35] he says. "I didn't want to be different, see? This was my — All my years in the United States, since 1951 — that's 34 years already — I have tried to emulate the Americans, to be like — I wanted to be part, I want to be like the Americans. I tried, — God knows I tried long to get rid of my accent. Of course, I still have an accent and jokingly I said, 'I never had an accent until I came to the United States.'

"But I imagined that I didn't want to be fingered, you know. 'He is this' like saying, you know, 'He walks around with ripped pants,' or 'He's very, very poor,' or 'He begs,' or something. You know, I wanted to be part of the society, of the idea of melting pot, you know, melting into the society, being part. This is what I tried very, very much."

But just 40 years earlier, no one really wanted to listen. Mordechai, Resnik and other survivors were often surprised, sometimes even offended, by the people now willing to listen. After all, they say, their experiences are no less gruesome, no less life-threatening in 1985 than they were in 1945.

"I don't think that Greenvillians knew that I am a survivor," Resnik says. "I've never advertised it until about eight years ago when I started talking about it. In fact, I had at one time — which I still have it — this shyness or perhaps you could call it shame — that I am a survivor. I don't like people to say, 'Well, he is a survivor.' Somehow, I — I don't know what it is in me ... I remember when I came to New York and I went — young people my age — people would point. And I could see fingers, literally. And it was, 'Hey, this guy is —'. And I could overhear."

The first time he ever discussed his experiences, Bramy Resnik spoke to a high school class. A friend from the Jewish temple in Kinston, N.C., where the Resniks were members invited Bramy Resnik to speak.

"And one of the students heard that I had been a survivor. And they did a topic on World War II," Resnik recalls. "And the student, you know, rather than write a paper on World War II — she decided that she'd invite me to talk about it. And for the first time I had to talk in front of a group of people, telling them what I am.

"This was about eight years ago. I remember distinctly that I walked into the room and the first thing I said, 'I am a survivor.' And I wanted to say, 'So don't you ever say anything about it.' But, of course, I controlled myself because I had this chip on my shoulder which I still partially have that — what can I help it? You know, this is me.

"And slowly and slowly, I talked about it. In fact, I almost refused the second year. But then my wife convinced me. (She said), 'These are kids. They have to know about it.' And, of course, being an educator, I agreed with her. These are kids. They have to be told. Someone has to tell them.

Even the children of survivors feel this quiet sense of responsibility to make sure people know what happened to their parents, why, where and how it happened, and how it affected both the survivors and their offspring.

Erica Hekler, and her older brother, Donald, believe the story must be told while there are still survivors alive to tell it. And, both are determined to better understand how the experiences of their parents, Ursula and Norman Hekler, have influenced their own lives and development. Donald has spent years in study, reading and some psychotherapy in an effort to come to grips with the past. Erica, named for her mother's sister who died in the Holocaust, has explored her feelings with friends and looked for answers at public lectures and study programs.

Donald Hekler says he was in his late 20s or early 30s before he realized the difference the Holocaust had made in his own life.

"This is embarrassing. The therapist I was seeing mentioned to me about the facts that I was a child of a survivor," he says.[36]

"See, the thing was, up until that point, that had always been a part of my life. That was normal and I didn't realize — you know, no one ever told me how abnormal it really is, and I don't mean that with a negative connotation, just, you know, the difference of it.

"And she suggested a book or two and, I think at that time, the whole concept or issue of children of survivors got to be popular. And there were some books written and that sort of thing. And either she mentioned to me or my mother brought them to my awareness at that point, but that therapist was the first person who really, you know, told me how unusual my background really is."

Perhaps people talk about the Holocaust now because "it's old enough now to be history to everybody," Donald says. "And, I think, also, a lot of the people who survived it, either as survivors or soldiers, whatever, realize that, you know, they are about to die. It's a very melodramatic way to say it, but, you know, their lives are getting to their ends and they want to make sure that this stuff is recorded, because a lot of it hasn't been."

Erica expounds her brother's feelings. "I can't remember the age, but I couldn't figure out why everyone else had grandparents and I didn't, and that's when I really realized, and I was mad and I told me I hadn't, and little things like that. And other children probably noticed that I was (different). And other children also noticed that my parents had accents. Of course, that was all a part of normal life to me and I've never heard their accents."

All through the studies of the Holocaust in which she has participated, Erica has tried to understand why.

"And no one has really ever come up with an answer to why," she says. "It was always, 'Well, you were the chosen people. You've always been the scapegoat.' I think, in a personal view, that for everything that happens on earth, we may not see the total picture. It's like a jigsaw puzzle and there are pieces missing, but I definitely think everything happens for a reason, but, yet, I cannot explain why that happened and I cannot see the reason behind it...

"Whatever I learned historically, I would go home and ask my parents, 'Did this happen to you? Is this true? Is this not true?' Sometimes historians have a way of throwing things a little bit out of proportion, maybe, or not — there's no personal aspect to history. History is cut and dried; when you have someone reliving an experience like Kristallnacht — what happened that night, what you did, how you nearly pulled through, what you felt, what your neighbors felt. That was just unbelievable to me "

"I felt at times as a child that my life was different, and it was, from other kids. And I was mad at my parents for being different, and I didn't like it at times.

"For all survivors and children of the survivors, I'm sure it's always Why?' I'm sure that question will always be there."

CHAPTER 9
THE NEXT GENERATION

Holocaust survivors who became parents have difficulty articulating just how much their children mean to them, and to the Jewish people. They sum up their feelings with statements like "She is my life."

Bramy Resnik, a survivor who lived to see a son and a daughter grow up, says it well:

"You see, to have a child now, after World War II, after the Holocaust, is to actually show to Hitler and his henchmen that: 'You did not succeed here. I was able to produce in spite of what you have tried to destroy.'"

So the children of survivors know they are special. After all, their parents are among only 75,000 Jews who lived to know freedom once again.

Donald Hekler, the oldest of three children born to Ursula and Norman Hekler, both survivors, was in his 30s before he connected adult feelings and experiences to his unusual parentage. He now lives in Annapolis, Md., working in sales for a wholesale distributor of bicycles and bicycle parts. Born in Asheville, he

He doesn't know whether his problems were alike, or different from, the common tensions between parents and adolescents. "I don't know about most people because, by that point, I was realizing that part of what was going on was the fact that I was brought by people ... who had very warped lives. And I didn't blame them for it, and I've never been angry at them for that. But I have this realization."

His problems continued until Hekler started seeing a psychologist. "I went to see one on a one-to-one basis for a time. And at that same time, was going to a group once a week. And the type of therapy ... was a combination of transactional analysis and Gestalt work, and it was really effective.

"One of the things I realized out of that work was that one of the reasons that I was mad at my parents was because they never told me they loved me the way I wanted them to. And, if I wanted to be happy with them, I was going to have to hear them the way they *were* doing it, not the way I wanted them to do it. It was things that they said like, 'Why are you wearing those jeans with the holes in the knee?' 'When are you going to get a haircut?' All those things. And when they do that, what they're saying is: 'I love you, and I'm concerned about you.' "

His parents never concealed their wartime experiences from him. Instead, the puzzle of their unusual past came together as Hekler picked up bits and pieces of their history, and the history of the Holocaust. "What I know is sort of a lifetime's accumulation of, you know, this fact one day, another fact next week."

'I know what the hell happened to them," he says. Then, he reconsiders. "There's all sorts of things I just don't know. And all sorts of family I don't know. And there are all these photo albums full of people. I don't know who they are and that sort of thing. And I know all these people who come from families that have umteen aunts and uncles and a zillion cousins, who come from families that have always been very much the opposite."

He was about 10 when he first connected his parents with the Holocaust in an historical sense. "We were in Europe," Hekler says. "It was their first trip back and I was about 10 and Hedy (one of his two sisters) was about 5, I guess. ... They went back to Europe and they took us with them. It was a long trip. I'm not sure why they went at that point. This is like in '56, I guess.

"It was an extensive trip. We went all over Europe, went to Israel. I saw some of the — I saw the house my father grew up in and visited some relatives and met my uncle and aunt and his brother and sister-in-law for the very first time.

"And while we were in Holland, we went to the Anne Frank house. My mother was raised in Holland. And she was hiding at the same time as the Franks, two blocks down and one block over, literally. And I don't know what that place is like now, but then it was a memorial and there were all these, you know, all your standard hideous Holocaust pictures all over the wall and that was when it was really presented to me.

"That's a real milepost in my life, and it stands out so much that, if there was a realization previously to that, I don't remember it. But, you know, I look back on it with some amazement because here I was 10 years old and I was seeing these incredible pictures and that was presented to me as 'us.'

"I'm kind of amazed at my reaction now because the first time I saw it, it was like looking at something in a museum that you have no connection with. It was pictures of emaciated dead people in a ditch, one of those mass graves. And, you know, your standard 8-by-10 glossy, black-and-white photograph. The place was covered with them."

He cannot remember how he reacted. "I think I really sublimated a lot. ... I think, you know, as a 10-year-old, I had to. I did not feel any sort of, you know, consciously feel any sort of insecurity. I mean, I was with my parents. We were staying with my mother's aunt, who was a stern woman, but she had a nice house. ... I think that my parents, all of a sudden, got a lot older than I thought they were. ... And there was this incredibly serious stuff in my parents' lives that I didn't know was there before, and we talked about it more after that and it's hard for me to separate out the conversation I had on that trip and then one I had later when I was 17, back in Europe again, back in Israel again with them. And because some of the revelations that have come to me there with two strangers because I was sitting there with my uncle, a man I don't know, because ... I don't think I've seen him a half dozen times in my life. And sitting there with my father, who would momentarily regress to a different relationship, you know, a different time in his life remembering things about relatives that I've never heard of before, because his family was completely gone, and events that I've never heard about, things between the two of them. ... It was like dealing with different people, you know, dealing with a man I had never seen before."

Yet it was much, much later when the pieces of the puzzle began to come together and Hekler seriously thought about the effect of his parents' experiences on his own life.

"Well, I began to have a lot more compassion for myself because I'm my own harshest critic still, and at that point, I would really give myself a hard time for what I thought were my shortcomings. And that was something, that insight, you know, that my upbringing was different, that I was being brought up by people who had, through no fault of their own, become — oh, 'emotional cripple' seems like such a melodramatic word, but I don't know another way to put it. But being brought up with people who had no childhood basically, no chance to go from being little kids to being adults. The transition was just one of fear and horror. And so beginning to realize that I was brought up by those people, you know, gave me a bit of a break and saying, 'Wait a minute. You know there are some reasons that you're doing this stuff.'

"And I think that's how it started, but really the true insight I think happened just a couple of years ago, when I really had created a more emphathic view of my parents. That enabled me to really soften my view of them."

Had his father had a youth, not been in a camp, not lost most of his family, maybe, Hekler says, his dad would be more open. "He went through some experiences that I can't comprehend going through myself. The same thing with my mother. They both lost virtually their entire families and they were really young, 14 years old, 15 years old, that sort of thing. My father escaped from Vienna when he was 15 years old and never saw his parents again."

"And they've had to incorporate this incredible horror, and fear, and sadness into their lives, and you know, if they hadn't gone through all that — well, there would be a larger support group for them. I think my father would be a little more relaxed about some subjects. You know, he's never had anyone to fall back on, ever. And maybe a bit more easy-going. ... And I don't know how to put that into a better description, but he's a very hard-working person, almost to the point of being a workaholic.

"Mother, Lord knows what she would have been like if that hadn't happened because the woman is brilliant. She has no schooling."

To Donald Hekler, it seems that part of his parents was lost in the Holocaust. With his mother, it's a youthful, gay side that comes out only in snatches. With his father, he says, it's as though his ability to be openly loving was wounded by the Holocaust.

"He just never had a chance to show fear or show love ... to parents and that sort of thing. I think what happened to him was so shattering and you know, losing his family so precipitously and then   He must have gone through years of not knowing anything about what happened to them, and then there was an incident in the camp he was in where some people were rounded up off the streets, brought in, shot and then he was one of the people that was instructed to pick them up and pile them up like cord wood. And my father has a very morbid fear of death and I think it stems from that.

"And I think he's really closed off portions of it himself and I think that's why he's so tentative sometimes when I hug him "

After therapy, self-analysis and some good years in closer communication with his parents, Hekler says he now understands why he has had emotional problems and why *who* he becomes is much more important to his parents than to most.

"I realize now that I'm a symbol of something for them in terms of, you know, continuation of life, of future, and all those symbols.

"And, I don't want to sound like I'm blaming them because I'm not. It's just, you know, fate. ... And, if anything, it's given me a greater appreciation for my own life than a lot of people I think the Anne Frank house in Amsterdam. The memory of the conversation still is vivid almost 10 years later. Hekler, 25, sits in her apartment in a complex in the heart of Atlanta, Georgia, and tries to remember exactly what she and her mother, Ursula, said to each other that day.

"It was very quiet. I'm sure I was, too,"[39] she says. "And we went up into the attic which was where they lived, and we peered out a window and we saw a clock tower, a church clock tower And, I think, we heard the bells, and my mother said, 'Oh, I heard those same bells.'

"And, then, we walked down the street where my mother had been in hiding, and I said, 'Which house was it that you were in hiding?' And she couldn't remember."

Like her brother, Hekler remembers that her parents made certain she understood the significance of the trip. But they did not tell her how to respond to what she saw and learned.

"I asked several questions: 'How old were you? What happened?' I got very few answers. But it just seems too amazing because here we were in modern-day Europe, the hustle and bustle of the big city, but, yet the city, Amsterdam itself, as a whole, is preserved. ... It was so hard for me to believe that this modern city with its modern ethics and modern governmental policies, its liberated ideas, could possibly have harbored such evil and such injustice in the past."

She was 16 when she visited Amsterdam. Her questions about the Holocaust began long before then, however.

"It's not as if it were a hidden fact and then, all of a sudden, 'boom,' they told me this. I suppose it had been part of all of my life. It just didn't happen overnight. I guess I just put two-and-two together and things started coming together that I was a little bit different, and that they were definitely different."

By the time Erica Hekler was born, her family could afford to travel even more extensively than when Donald Hekler was a child. As they had at home, her parents again worked to help their children appreciate art, music and literature.

"I think my parents just wanted to show us the world and bring out all the beauty and show us what was good and what to appreciate," Erica Hekler says.

"If I had personally been through what they had been through, I would want to live life to its fullest, and I would want to show my children the beauty in the world, including nature and other cultures and people, and would want them to appreciate and understand what's going on around them."

Being the daughter of two survivors has not cast shadows over her life. "It's almost made me special in a strange way," she says. "I think my parents have strived to give me everything that they could possibly give me, not materialistically."

Friends' reactions to her unusual background vary, Hekler says. "I have several friends who are Southern Baptists and they are shocked and amazed. They don't even know that people like me and my parents exist. They have no knowledge of it. First of all, they don't know much about Judaism, period. And that this (the Holocaust) is a fact of history is just *history* to them. They don't feel it's life "

Her parents were so cheated of normal childhood experiences that Hekler never felt comfortable asking her mother's advice in simple matters such as which dress she should wear to a school dance. Yet whenever she studied the Holocaust in school, Hekler tried to connect it to her own life.

Today she blames the Holocaust on the citizens of pre-World War II Germany, and the difficult economic situation that nation confronted. But she studied German in high school, later becoming so proficient in the language that she majored in it as a college student at Tulane University in New Orleans. When she graduated, she moved home for awhile, but disliked High Point and longed to live in a larger city. So she moved to Atlanta. First, she pounded pavements, then landed a job in a restaurant where she hoped to make a career in the "wonderful world of gourmet food." With a characteristic shrug, Hekler grins and admits:

"Unfortunately, it didn't work out. And I took the next available job I could get which was a clerk and then I moved to office manager."

She still sees her parents' values and their experiences influencing her life.

"As far as money goes, also, my parents had always taught me not to spend what you don't have. And I know that when they came to the United States, they were broke. They had nothing.

"And I remember my father told me that someone in our family had told my mother that my father would never make anything out himself. And when I asked him, I said, 'Well, didn't that hurt your feelings? Didn't you get depressed? Weren't you mad?' He said, 'No.' He said, 'I knew that wasn't true. I knew I'd make it.'

"So that has stuck with me even though there have been times when I've said, 'Oh, my God, my friends are doing so much better than I am,' it's like that's not true. I'll make it. I'm a smart individual. I mean, I'm a good individual, and I'll make it. Success is not only money. It's being happy in your job and feeling productive, which I do feel very much right now."

Like their parents, Donald and Erica Hekler share a unique sense of history, of background, and of the hope that their births represent to survivors who lost so many they loved. It is a common theme among the children of survivors. Whether they learn exactly who their parents are just through listening or by asking direct questions, many of the children grow up feeling part of a history they never experienced. They also understand, and in some cases accept the burden that history places on them to achieve, to become all that their parents never had a chance to be.

Such a sense of responsibility seems to be a little easier to shoulder if it is shared. As survivors have formed local support groups and nationwide networks, so have their children. Now in her 30s, Florence Goemaat says her life as a child was easier in northern New Jersey because there were other children of survivors in her neighborhood. As an adult, she has plugged into the growing network of children of survivors and works to make certain that her three young children, who are aged 10, 7 and 4, understand their Jewish roots even though her husband, John, is not Jewish.

Her parents, Morris and Sally Leibowitz Niedzwiedz, told Goemaat and her younger sister, Barbara, about their youth and about World War II. Her mother is Romanian, her father Polish.

She was born in Bergen-Belsen, once a Nazi concentration camp and later a displaced persons camp.

"My mother was one of six children,"[40] Goemaat says. "She was the only one to have survived. Her father did survive; he remarried and had another family of five children and is now the grandfather to over 30 children. ... But my mother was the only one to survive from the first family.

"My father was one of three (children). And he and his sister survived. She's married and she lives in Israel and she has no children. He, of course, had two children. But, as I say, there was no contact. She lived in Israel; he lived here. So, as I say, growing up was sad for us. It really was. That will always stay with me. Because there was just the four of us."

Unlike the Heklers, Goemaat's parents were not affluent enough to travel. But she longs to see Israel and to show it to her husband and children. In summer 1984, she and her husband, who works for AT&T already were planning and saving for a family trip to Israel, which they hope to make in 1989.

"We grew up in an area of northern New Jersey where there were other survivor families, a bilingual neighborhood." Goemaat says. "Lots of people from Europe, survivors, Jews and Gentiles Russian, Ukrainian, Polish. And so we all had this common European background and a kind of socio-economic neighborhood where one group of people was moving out and another group of people was moving in. And we were the other — the refugees, really."

Though her parents talked about the Holocaust, Goemaat says, it was not until the trial of Adolph Eichmann, which was heavily covered by the media, that she really understood what her parents had experienced.

"I think, at that time, I became aware of the historical

what ultimately was done to them, because they were very young people at the time.

"They were young enough to have survived and old enough to have taken care of themselves. ... When they began to empty out the camps in the mid-1940's and early '45, they (the Nazis) ultimately marched everyone toward Germany to cover up their tracks. And that's why they both wound up being liberated in Germany at two different camps in '45. And they met after the liberation, were married in Germany, have a German civil marriage certificate, and I have a German birth certificate, and (they) were waiting to go to the United States or Israel. And it just so happened that their names came up on the quota to go the United States in 1950.

"Perhaps it was better that they never took the opportunity to sit us down and explain the experience; rather they just — talked about it. They were not that closed-mouthed about it. They talked about it. ... And I don't know when I became aware of ... the significance of the numbers. But somewhere along the line I did." (Her father has a number tattooed on his arm.)

"Just through the years, the bits and pieces kind of came together. And, as I say, it was not an English-speaking home; it was Yiddish speaking. That's because they're from two different — they are natives from two different countries. ... And Yiddish was the common language they spoke to each other."

Goemaat feels admiration, not anger, when she thinks of her parents. "You know, I've seen my mother cry so often. She's an emotional person and raised emotional, highly emotional children. I think that I emotionally unwind every time I see a film or an old newsreel of what went on. ... And I marvel at how my mother, who was just 19 at the time of liberation. ... It amazes me. She's a very small woman. But she's a very strong person and truly a survivor in every sense of the word.

"I suppose I blame the times," Goemaat says. "I don't know if Hitler would have evolved. He may have lived, but certainly not have evolved into the person he evolved into had it not been —" She stops short, then finishes the thought. "The times of every civilization produce a Napoleon, a Caesar. The times just allowed it, allowed him to develop into the kind of person that he was.

"You know, I often asked my mother, 'How did you just stand by? How did everyone just stand by and let this happen?' Well, the question was: Where was there to go? See, there was nowhere for them to go. And, I think, ultimately they all said: 'Well, maybe if we live through this, there will be some place to go.'"

Goemaat moved to North Carolina in the late 1970s when her husband's work brought the family here. She moved again with her family to Warren, N.J., in 1986. She has a bachelor's degree in political science and a master's degree in library science, so questions of history, issues that require painstaking research, will always interest her. When her own children are older, she hopes to help them understand what the Holocaust means in their own family history. As they grow up, she is emphasizing involvement in the local Jewish community, and in religious life, in hopes of helping her offspring to come to know and love their Jewish roots as much as she does.

"What makes us special?" she asks, when questioned about being the child of survivors. "You know, there must be a cementing force. I suppose a cementing force would be what our parents went through. ... As a child of a person who was the only one who survived in her family, she (her mother) is perpetuating through me, and my children are perpetuating through me. ... I suppose if I were to take the view that I was no longer interested in Judaism and did nothing to practice it, well, it wouldn't be very long until everyone lost interest.

"I don't think any of us should ever be so content with our lives to think that nothing like this could ever happen again. I truly believe that. You know, I think it's very easy to feel that these things won't happen again, but I don't believe that.

"The history of man is a history of scapegoats. I mean, we're forever blaming one another for, you know, what happens. We're not the reason; somebody else is the reason. So I think it's a whole history of scapegoats. But Jewish history, it just goes on and on a history of scapegoats. Blame them and blame them. As I said, it's a wonder we still are around."

CHAPTER 10
THE LIBERATORS

When the revelation began, the first witnesses were unprepared. Like so many other patriotic idealists, they were soldiers serving their countries by fighting in World War II. Death was part of combat.

But when the first Allied troops marched into Nazi concentration camps, they confronted a set of rules for civilian death unlike anything they had ever known.

Sgt. Carlton Raper of Pleasant Garden, N.C., had been warned before he arrived at the main gate at Dachau. It is not a pleasant place, his captain had said. Typhus is rampant. Beware of giving surviving prisoners food, because many are too ill to eat.

Lt. Glenn Farthing, who lives in Advance, N.C., had heard the stories of death in concentration camps. But not a single thing these men heard before entering Dachau prepared either Farthing or Raper for what they saw there.

From the beginning of the Third Reich, the Nazis had built transit camps, concentration camps, extermination camps and centers. Some were small; some large. There were, at least, 20 story brings the memory to life once again, opens up the past, and uncovers all the questions of why. Raper's open, distinctly Southern farm-boy face loses its natural color. His eyes look distant. He tries to explain.

"The most of us had already been witness to death and destruction on a scale that boggled the mind to the breaking point. Still, we were not prepared for the nightmarish horror and absolute evil of a concentration camp," Raper said in a letter.[41]

In an interview, he went into deeper, gruesome detail.

"You have to sort of be in the army to understand these things," he says.[42] "But I was in an engineer combat group. ... It was a headquarters group which meant that there was a full colonel in command of my little company. I'm talking about 120 men and 68 officers. ... And we had anywhere from three to five battalions attached to our group's headquarters at all times. We were principally pontoon bridge builders."

The hatred of Jews that helped build the concentration camp is as alien an emotion to this man as the word "anti-Semitism" would have been to a youthful Raper while he was growing up in Greensboro. "I never knew the word until after the war, I don't think," he explains.

Sure, he knew Jewish people, but not on that basis. "I went to school with Jewish people. .. I have been living around and among Jewish people, and Negro people, Greek people. Greensboro has been a — well, I guess it's been fortunate in a way we've had a cross-section of the world here.

But Raper never thought much about what it meant to be Jewish until after World War II. "They were just somebody else, you know. ... But, I knew we had some rich Jews — I knew the Cones were here. I went to school with the Cones. But we had some Jews that were not so rich who ran a delicatessen store or had a little tailor shop. ... I mean they were just like the rest of us."

Just like the rest of the folks he knew. That's what Raper thought everyone else thought, too, until he saw Dachau in April 1945.

About a year before he entered the camp, Raper first began to hear stories about the Jews who had suffered in concentration camps. "In my outfit," he says, "there were three Jewish boys, European Jews. They had escaped the Holocaust, which I didn't even know about. I got on fairly good terms with one of them, and one day, he asked me, just out of the blue, if I'd ever heard of Dachau. And I said, 'Well, I may have, but I don't know.' And I didn't. I don't know if it was from him or other sources that I started hearing all these atrocity stories about the concentration camps. ... That's about it until I finally got to see one."

Raper pulls a map out of an envelope he has brought with him. He places his company's location on the map. His unit's job was to support the work of the division that liberated Dachau. Raper cannot remember the number of that division, or exactly how long it had been since Dachau's liberation when he went in.

He went to Dachau at the suggestion of his company commander. Twenty-five to 30 of the 120 men in his company also went, in spite of the warnings that diseases were rampant in the camp.

When he went, Raper stayed less than three hours, but will carry the scars of that 180 minutes to his grave. "I'd never seen anything like it. Now I had seen dead bodies before, believe me, plenty of them, American and German. And if you're like me, you'll never get used to death. It's something you recoil from. But I never expected to see the sorrow of a place like Dachau. There's no way I can describe it, really."

His voice cracks. He pulls out a worn copy of a letter to the editor of the *Greensboro Daily News*. It is more an essay than a letter, but it offers a fleeting image of what he saw. With great difficulty, Raper wrote the letter in 1978, after reading a review of the book, *Deliverance Day: The Last Hours at Dachau*. As he pushes the copy of the letter closer, Raper's hand trembles, his eyes mist. He is trying to explain. "I state (it) in that just about as well as I can," he says.

Inside the barracks most of the prisoners were too weak or too deranged to show any elation at being liberated. They seemed to want to hold onto their bunks as children hold onto security blankets. Some few inspected their

A zombie-like creature in prison garb, perhaps a trusty, fed bodies into the crematoria. As I recall, there were three furnaces going and he used a meat hook type staff to pull bodies off the stacks of bodies and onto a low bed steel trundle with steel wheels. He would then open a furnace door and push the body, trundle and all, into the flames. He worked slowly, but methodically, alternating from one furnace to another.

The prisoners were perhaps from every nation of Europe; there were even some Turks. I remember that most, aside from Jews, seemed to be Greeks, Poles, Slavs, Romanians and Hungarians .

So this was my experience at Dachau, and for weeks afterwards, I felt unclean, permeated with the stench and filth of the place. And no matter how many showers I took it would not go away. Perhaps it was a moral stench I was trying to wash away, and I confess, it has not entirely left me yet.[43]

It is this sense of evil, a horror both allowed to happen and one in which he became an unwitting participant, that still haunts Carlton Raper.

"You know," he says, "we're cousins to the Germans; I mean people of English heritage, and I feel like these people are so close to me racially, 'How could you have done such a thing?' And it's still an enigma to me, and I don't know. I don't know why, and I tried to find out why. And I cannot even imagine how they got into such a state.

"Apparently Hitler was able to lead the German people on a colossal ego trip. And I still can't believe they knew what was going on, but they ... must have. They must. They couldn't have hid all this — no way."

He says he doesn't understand, then tries to explain. He says he cannot believe the German people knew what was going on, then doubles back, changes his mind, and says the Germans must have known. They must have known about the camps, and maybe they knew about the genocide now known as "The Final Solution."

"I don't see how you can just hate the Jews, or anybody for that matter, enough to railroad them off, and gas them, and put them through the treatment and all that. It's just incredible. It's just —I don't know. I can't understand it." Raper says those three words, "I don't know," over and over.

* * *

Glenn Farthing echoes Carlton Raper's thoughts.

"It was really hard to believe," Farthing says.[44] "We knew that several things were occurring, and you expect them to occur during war time. But, insofar as people being caged or cooped up like these people were, and starved to death, it was really beyond our imagination."

Farthing marched into Dachau about a week before World War II actually ended in Germany. During the war, he was an infantry officer, stationed in France, then Germany. Later he was attached to the 7th Army Headquarters.

"We were continually moving. I joined the 7th Army Headquarters in Darmstadt just south of Frankfurt and then moved with them down through the Bavaria Province of Germany. At the time I got into Dachau, we were actually stationed at Augsburg."

Farthing ruffles one hand through a still-thick shock of silvery-gray hair. He is sitting in the comfortable living room of his suburban Greensboro home. His son watches football nearby. Pictures of his wife, Martha, his other three children and his grandchildren decorate living-room end tables. A coffee-table picture book, *The Scenic Wonders of America,* sits on another table. It is quiet, peaceful, a calm Sunday afternoon in a peaceful Southern city. Farthing, 62 when I interviewed him, since has retired from his job as a mechanical engineer with a major Southeastern textile firm. He now lives in Advance. His life is settled, secure. But, still, he cannot forget Dachau.

"Being attached to the 7th Army Headquarters, I was a day or two behind the actual liberation of Dachau. But I went into Dachau not knowing at all what was there.

"I had heard of concentration camps. And then, having just learned that we had just liberated one, I made it a point to get up there as soon as possible. We had so little information that all I knew was that it was a place where the Germans kept prisoners of the Jewish faith and also political, or so-called enemies of the state.

I knew it would be a barbed-wire enclosure. But I really was not prepared for the crematorium and such.

"The first thing I saw as we got into the actual confines of the camp were the cages where the SS troops kept their big, vicious dogs. The dogs were still lying where our troops had shot them a day or so earlier. ... Then the next thing was the walking skeletons, you might say, the hundreds of people who were so emaciated. In fact, many of them were too far gone to save. They were dying at a rate of 20 or 30 a day when we liberated Dachau.

"I guess the next thing that really caught my attention and was quite distressing and horrible was the tremendous mound of bodies — naked bodies, just skin and bones, at the crematorium. The Germans just hadn't gotten around to cremating them.

"Near the bodies — the Germans being a very methodical type people — were articles of clothing: trousers in one pile; shoes in another pile; jackets in another pile; and so forth. Then the next thing that caught our attention was a line of boxcars on the rail siding in the camp. In these boxcars were more bodies. The Germans had thrown a layer of bodies, some lime, and then another layer of bodies   "

Again the memory is a recollection of horror stacked upon horror, hate piled atop hate.

"Of course, I had seen death and injury and suffering. But persecution on this scale — in fact, at all, this was my first experience. And it was very distressing, very horrible to contemplate."

Months later, Farthing returned to his hometown, Valle Crucis in the mountains of Western North Carolina. He brought with him photographs, other memorabilia to prove what he had seen.

"I had no hesitation in telling them what I had seen. ... I made no attempt to conceal it at all. In fact, I would say, I was interested in letting people know what I had actually seen. ... Well, the fact is that it is such a terrible thing to have happened, and it's pretty much unbelievable.

"Today, some people refuse to believe it. And there are people who claim that it didn't happen. But obviously, it did. And we need to do everything we can to be sure that people are advised of the truth and to understand how things like this can develop and snowball unless they are nipped in the bud or unless effective action is taken in the early stages of this type of atrocity."

Farthing doesn't think of himself as either an historian or a political analyst. A quiet, pragmatic man, he is willing to talk about his experiences mainly because he believes others can learn from what he saw.

"I appreciate the fact that I did have the opportunity to be there and see it first-hand," he says. "I believe it is hard for an ordinary person to grasp the extent of what happened there. But, having seen it, there can be no doubt.

"I don't think it basically changed my character, my outlook on life. But it made me aware of, let's say, human weakness and the fact that things can develop that are really too horrible to contemplate.

"I think we probably are naive. I think, due to our living in a free country where we can speak out without fear of government retribution, that we tend to feel that the same situation exists in other countries," Farthing explains.

"I think we need to be on the alert for things happening in other countries, such as Ethiopia, Laos and Vietnam, where opponents of the totalitarian government are being eliminated. ... I believe that similar things are occurring in Afghanistan, for example. And I believe we, as a free people, as the most important country in the free world, have an obligation to speak up and let the oppressors know in that case that we don't go along with it; that we don't want it to happen; and that we'll take whatever actions we can to prevent it."

So the youth of the United States must be educated to realize that a smaller version of the Holocaust, systematic repressions and brutal murders, can occur in any country, but especially under a totalitarian communist regime.

"It is incumbent on all of us to understand that those things can happen," Farthing says. "And that we must be on guard, and alert, and speak out in opposition early in the game, when something like that is taking place.

"By neglect, by simply turning our eyes away from things like that, they can grow to the point where stopping becomes virtually impossible.

"I believe that's what happened in Germany."

CHAPTER 11
TURNING TO THE ULTIMATE

Four decades have elapsed since Allied troops liberated the last of Hitler's concentration camps. To this day, survivors pause, looking back to search a map of their memories and find the road marker directing them to God. Most eventually turn away from the past, facing the future without an answer. Others never search, and the Jewish part of their lives becomes a public display with little private meaning. Some run in another direction, seeking answers in other religions.

Eva Weiner still searches. When she first emerged from 18 months of hiding in Poland during the war, Weiner says she still prayed.

"I was a very big believer. I loved the synagogue. My husband still goes every single day, but not because we are religious now. I question God. Where was he when we were praying and screaming and crying out to him, 'Help us'?[45]

"Why did he pick only us? I know they was killing a lot of people, millions of people got killed. But they was fighting for their life. We couldn't fight for our lives. And that's the difference. I ask God still today ... where was he?"

If it happened today, things would be different. She would be tougher. Other Jews would be tougher, Weiner says. She clenches her right hand, then her left.

"If I would have to live through my life today, I would fight. I would kill you before you kill me. Or you would kill me before I kill you. But I wouldn't go like, like cattle to the grave to be killed.

But we were so scared. We believed, and we talked to God. We would believe in God and God couldn't do anything like that to us. Why? Why not you? Why only me?

"I think what we have to do right now is to educate the young kids not to have grudges against each other because any human being, any color he is, black or white, or red, or blue, is human. Is born. ... Why should these people (be) cut off from their lives before (their) time and for what? What really the Jews doing so bad in this world, that they are so hated? That's the question, why are we so hated? What did we do so bad in this world?"

Others ask the same question in different ways. Some reclaim their Jewishness in Zionism. Others mold their religious lives gently, bowing to convention and maintaining synagogue membership, but only for propriety's sake. Others reject their Jewish roots, seeking solace in Judaism's theological descedant Christianity.

"Yes, I prayed," Bramy Resnik says of his days in a concentration camp.[46] "I'd say, 'Oh, God, please help me.' I was not religious in the very religious sense. I didn't say a special prayer from the Bible. I would just, say, pray between myself and God, you know, my good friend. He's my good friend.

"And I'd say, 'God, how can you do this to me?' You know, 'Look at me. Look at my father, my cousin, I don't even see Mother. I haven't seen Mother in a year. I mean, what are you doing?' Almost talking to him.

"It didn't help. He didn't reply. And, of course, in my naive way and, perhaps, in reality at that time, I did not think there was a God. ... But, perhaps, if I did, I'd say he had abandoned me. When you saw little children, innocent children, a week old, being ripped apart by the Germans from limb to limb, literally, where you take a piece of paper and rip apart, in two — when you see that, when you see the other twin thrown under a tank, and another soldier holding a half of another human body, a little human body that's only about a foot and a half long, almost two

"I doubted at the time. I doubt that God was at his work, if there is a God. I still have doubts that there is a god, a superior power. ... Don't get me wrong. I want to believe there is a superpower, not superpower, there is a supreme power that guides us. But, often I have that difficulty to accept that there is a supreme power, because if there is one, why does he allow a child who walked down the street, whether he is Jewish or non-Jewish, today (to be) hit by a car?

"Why does God allow that? ... What kind of sins had that child committed to suffer? You think about the poor little child that was born — I don't know what city it was — and the baboon heart was implanted in her. Why? Why, if God is so perfect? And God is perfect. God cannot be imperfect because if God were imperfect, man would look for another god. Right? So, if God is perfect, why does he allow that poor child to suffer? It's only a week or two weeks old. Just born. And the same thing. ... Why did God permit for these two little twins, neighbors of ours, born and the Germans to take and kill them? I mean, this is just unheard of, to take and rip it apart?

"How can a human being do that? Even in a stupor, in a drunken state, a human being wouldn't do that. Of course, the rationalization today is, 'Well, it was their job.' That is a job? That is a job. Fine. Let's say theirs became a job to kill. But to kill with lust? That is not killing anymore. That is insanity."

* * *

It is the insanity of everything she experienced in the 11 months she spent in Auschwitz that haunts Klari Hermann Kletter.

Kletter is a pretty woman with a mane of gray-streaked, ash-blonde hair, wide blue eyes and a fondness for heavy gold bracelets and long, gold necklaces. The 55-year-old cannot tell her story of the Holocaust unemotionally. Her eyes well with tears when she speaks of the loss of her father, Bernard; her brother, Michael, and more than two-thirds of her father's family. One of seven children, Bernard Hermann and his clan had lived in Rosvegovo, a town of several thousand in Czechoslovakia, near the border with Hungary, for almost 200 years. Kletter has almost nothing left of that heritage. Each of her father's siblings was married, and each had several children. Out of a family of at least 28 people, only Kletter, her other brother Joseph, her mother Helena (now anglicized to Helen) and five cousins survived the war.

When World War II began, Kletter was in grade school. "We were not really touched until 1944," she says.[47] "Of course, I did not know that Germany was losing the war. But by that time, starting in '42 or '43, I knew that there was a Russian front. And the Nazis would go through, the tanks and you know, I guess they were going to the Russian front. ... I remember that a group of Polish people were coming through in a bus. They were Christian people. ... And these were young people, all ages. But I don't remember any old people. I only remember young people. And they were barefooted, and it looked like they picked them up from one street and stuck them into buses. And, I remember that we had a vineyard, and it was in the fall. And what I remember is that we threw them a lot grapes, meat, like ham and homemade bread.

"I did not know that these people will eventually end up in concentration camps; nor did they, those people, know."

The Hermanns were farmers and vineyard owners. Helena Hermann's Romanian roots were a religious mixture of Christianity and Judaism. Bernard Hermann was reared a Jew. Though her mother converted before the Nazis marched into Rosvegovo, Klari Kletter's religious education was an amalgamation of her parents' training. She remembers attending both a Jewish temple and a Roman Catholic church.

When the Nazis took her family away, Kletter says she was so young that "I didn't really understand why they took me."

Forty years later, she still does not understand. "I know about the Depression. I know about World War I. I know the people were poor. I know there was tremendous inflation in Germany. And yet, is this an excuse? I don't know. We were the scapegoats. We were farmers and we owned a vineyard. We were not bankers like Hitler said. I lived in a small town of 4,000 people. I rode the horses. I worked the horses. I ran through the river. It was like

"Everything was all right. Everything was just fine. And it was like overnight. It was so sudden. All of a sudden. It's just like they just didn't give you any time."

The Nazis marched in, gave Kletter's family two to three hours to pack.

"They came to the door, and they took us together," she recalls. "And then they separated us in Auschwitz."

They were transported in a boxcar. "And I remember that there was no room to even sit down. There was just people on top of people. I was with the whole family. And I remember something comes to my mind, it comes always to my mind. There is a sunset. You know, at that time, my father already must have known that in Poland the Jews were being killed. And if you are going east, that was sure death. And there was a sunset. And my father said, 'Oh, children, don't worry about anything. We are going west.' And west meant Germany, and, you know, that you had a better chance to survive."

It was only a fleeting chance for the Hermanns, however. The advance of the Russian army into Nazi-occupied territory forced the Nazis to take the Hermanns through Germany on the transport. But from there, they were taken to Auschwitz.

"My mother and I were put on the same side. My mother was real young, you know. I was only 14, and my mother was maybe 32. She was a young woman, and she went with the survivors. ... The right was the life line and the left was the crematorium."

But Kletter still had no idea where she was. "As we walked by the fence, we saw these people in striped clothes and barefooted, or they had, like wooden shoes. And they had no hair. They were all shaved. And we thought that maybe these people were crazy. ... So they were standing by the fence and looking at us. They were silent, and we walked past them. Of course, at this point, we were taken into this room, shaved and taken away our clothes. And the ones they gave us was stripes, coarse and drab."

Kletter and her mother never were tattooed with numbers like so many other Auschwitz prisoners. "I was supposed to die," Kletter explains. A protective block leader in her barracks and a quirk of fate saved her life.

The leader's name was Vera. "I always remember her," Kletter says. "And I guess probably she helped that I'm here ... (Josef)

Mengele would come, and she would sort of hide us, me and my mother.

"He came to the block and ... did one thing — right, left, right left. The ones on the left we knew would die. He came as close to me as you."

Life continued in a dull monotony of pain, confusion, degradation and fear until one night late in November. "We heard gunshots, and we did not know what it was — We figured maybe there was fighting, some kind of fighting. We went out and we heard it quite clearly. ... All of a sudden, they started to count out (prisoners). And they put us in the gas chamber. I was in the gas chamber, and I didn't know at first that I was. But I looked up and there were like — looked like a shower, see. And they give us, looked like a piece of soap. But we were naked, but a whole bunch of us. And there were little seats in there, something like that. I don't remember exactly. ... All of a sudden, somebody said something. And, I guess, my mother was smarter than I was, I guess. I saw panic on her face and I started to cry. And I said, 'Mommy, Mommy, I want to live. I'm so young. I want to live.' And Momma then said that I was just hitting my head against cement, whatever it was. 'Mommy, I don't want to die. Mommy.'

"And I remember my mother holding me. That's all I remember. And this was going on for maybe 10 or 15 minutes. And then, all of a sudden, a man came to the door. And he said, 'Are you crazy?' These are all young people. I can use them working in Germany.' He said, 'A transfer just came in for those people from Theresienstadt. Put them on the train. I can use them.' Out we went, back into the dresses. A loaf of bread. On the train. And if you think — if you think I'm still normal after this. You think for a minute that I am normal. And I had a lot of anger for years and years. ... I wanted to kill. I really did. For years. Oh, yes. I had a lot of anger in me."

Eventually, Kletter and her mother moved on to work in a munitions factory in Altenbourg. They stayed there until April 1945. The Allies began bombing, and the Nazis marched their prisoners on, away from the bombing, deeper into territory still controlled by the Germans. Kletter's memory of the details blurs at this point, but she vaguely recalls that a German officer told the soldiers guarding the prisoner group to set them free.

"And then, April 13, 1945, on a Friday, we were in the woods hiding. There was ferocious fighting going on. And we were up on a hill, like, and the bullets were just flying back and forth. My mother sort of lay down on top of me because I guess she thought she'd protect me like that. And we laid down in the leaves. And the shooting was going on for a long time, all night long. And somebody started to yell, 'There's a white flag. ... It looks like the English are occupying.' . And, all of a sudden, a man, which must have been a prisoner, too, from Hungary, a Hungarian man.

He started to yell, 'Children, come down, the Americans are here.' "

Kletter says the liberators were part of American troops headed by Gen. George Smith Patton. The troops gave Kletter chocolate, food rations, a blanket and a pair of army-issue boots. Eventually, she and her mother were taken to a makeshift hospital near where the American troops were bivouacked. The pair stayed there for about three months. When buses came to take Czechoslovakian prisoners home, she and her mother boarded a bus for Prague. There they learned that her father and one of her brothers were dead. They were reunited with Kletter's brother, Joseph, after he located their names on a list of survivors. Kletter never returned to her hometown. Her mother went back only to find that the Hermanns' property had been confiscated by Russian forces occupying the region.

Kletter continued to live in a hotel in Prague. Her mother, who suffered a nervous breakdown after the war, was in a hospital nearby. Kletter met her first husband, Paul Cerny, an American serviceman, while she was living in Prague. They married in 1946; she emigrated with him to the United States to New York City. They later divorced, and she remarried. Kletter, who asked that her second husband remain unidentified, moved to Greensboro in 1974 when her second husband's work brought the couple south. She has been legally separated from him for eight years.

Kletter has five children — four daughters and one son from her two marriages. In summer 1984, she sold her home in Greensboro and left the city for an extended trip to the Northeast and to Europe. She visited family in both places, but it was in Europe that she realized how much she has changed.

When she visited her brother Joseph and his wife in Duven-Echtz, West Germany, all her memories of the Holocaust came flooding back. "I walked everyday in the countryside," Kletter says. "As I walked, I walked by the fields, by the lakes. Here I am with all these Germans. And I said to myself as I'm walking around, 'This nation has so much to give, so much beauty, what happened? What kind of monster is a human being?' "

For Kletter, the first step to wholeness was to forgive. She lived with nightmares for 10 years after the war. She sought psychiatric help. Nothing worked until she told her story to a friend, in the early 1980s

"I had every kind of healing group that you can imagine; psychology, everything. Anything that I was able to put my hands on. ... 'I'm Okay, You're Okay', you name it, I bought it. ... I just wanted to be healthy. ... I have this friend of mine. ... And I told her the story. And she took my hand and she said to me, 'But you've got to forgive. Because if you don't forgive, you will never heal.' And I cried. I said, 'I can never forgive, I will never forgive.' And she said, 'Well, then, you'll be sick for all of your life.' And she took my hand. And I cried on her shoulder. And she said, 'The Lord. You have to believe in the Lord.' ... At this point, you see, I was already, Jesus was with me for a long time. Somehow, I don't know. Maybe it was because he was crucified. ... I don't know why. I started to read the Gospel. And, see, I found a lot of love. And I really needed somebody to teach me how to love. See, I did not, I didn't love."

Her friend's guidance, her own part-Christian roots and her need to forgive brought her to Christianity, Kletter says.

"Do you know what it means to forgive the Nazis?" her friend asked.

"And I said, 'Yes, I'm going to forgive them. And I'm going to forget them, Lord, and I'm going to forget about it. And I'm going to give it to you, and I'm going to let you — and you're going to have to heal me.' "

Kletter openly calls herself a "born-again Christian," and believes her conversion is what brought her out of deep misery and think it's very hard on them. When you don't forgive, that other person doesn't know. It hurts you, not them.

"Jesus said, 'When you become my followers, you will lose sometimes, your brothers, your sisters.' He said something on that order. 'They will hate you because you follow me.' "

Her conversion has meant coping with distance, strain, sometimes even the end of a friendship, Kletter says. But she believes the choice was the right one for her. If you ask her about the Holocaust, she fidgets with the heavy gold ring on her right hand, stumbles over the story. But if you ask her about being healed, she smiles, nods her head and says, "Oh, yes, absolutely." It is easy to be sure, she says. "Because I don't have the hatred, because I now have friends in Germany with whom I correspond. If that's not healing?"

But she is quick to say that the answer she found is not for every survivor.

"I feel that they are missing something. Sometimes I feel they are missing that inner peace and forgiveness. They may have it. I don't know. I still see my mother cursing and cussing."

Her mother never forgave the Nazis, Kletter says. "The funny thing is my mother became a real Jew and I became a Christian," she says. "My mother never forgave anybody. ... I know one thing. I had to forgive them. I can't forget. Too many memories. But I had to forgive. And I think I accomplished that."

How others find their peace is their affair, Kletter says. She willingly shares her own solution, but believes each must come to faith in his or her own way. "Because I feel basically there is only one God for all of us. I guess come call it Yahweh. Some call him Allah. The thing is that I can't judge. I really believe they're missing (something), but I feel, at the same time, that I have to respect every religion."

When I last talked with her, Klari Kletter planned to be baptized in the fall of 1985 at a small Roman Catholic church in New York City.

CHAPTER 12
SEEING JUSTICE DONE

Like Americans who followed the Nuremberg trials through newspapers and radio, Morris Kiel had trouble believing the scope of the Nazi atrocities revealed by the war criminals being tried at Nuremberg. He remembers very little about those crimes being reported in Europe and America during World War II. Even though some American leaders knew Jews and other prisoners were being slaughtered, Kiel says, many Allied servicemen and officers remained ignorant.[48]

"Well, as far as army records are concerned, I don't think there was too much about it," he says. "My experience and my knowledge came from — more from civilian sources than army sources. There were hints of what was happening. There were German refugees, if you want to call them German Jewish refugees, coming into this country starting in the 30s. And Kristallnacht was well publicized.

"But, once the war started, there seems to have been a lack, I would say, of publicity of Hitler's Final Solution* in comparison with many other things.

"Apparently from everything I've read since then, Roosevelt, Churchill, etcetera, were interested in winning the war, no matter what it cost as far as Jews, Poles or anybody else. ... At that time, I agreed, probably agreed with it. If I don't agree with it now, it's just a matter of hindsight."

---

*NOTE: The Final Solution was the Nazi plan to exterminate all Jews in

Looking back, Kiel shares the confusion of the men and women who survived the Holocaust. Just realizing that such evil is possible is difficult enough. Even tougher is realizing what that evil can turn into, how it can destroy and how democracies like the United States can let such a thing happen.

Kiel, 70, never saw Germany under Nazi domination. He was there after the Third Reich fell. His military career began in 1942 at Camp Croft, S.C., near Spartanburg. From there, be was sent to Fort Custer, Mich. "And then some intermediary camps while I was in a military police escort guard company guarding prisoners of war at Monticello, Ark.; Stuttgart, Ark." He did not arrive in Germany until September 1945.

"I received a commission in the Military Police and I was then transferred over to the Counter Intelligence Corps. ... They assigned me to a counter intelligence unit in Bamberg, Germany."

He attended a counterintelligence school at Oberammergau, assigned to the office as Bamberg Executive Officer. Two to three months later, he was appointed commanding officer of the Nuremberg field office.

When he arrived at Nuremberg, Kiel says, "The atmosphere was entirely different from the rest of the occupied territories. First, Nuremberg itself was a 10-mile international enclave under the jurisdiction of the American army. We had the police and the physical jurisdiction of handling the natives as well as the international Allied personnel. The 'Allied personnel', of course, were the Russians, the French, the English and the Americans, plus all other Allied countries, who were part of the international tribunal."

That tribunal was born in 1943 when the Allies, including Russia, Great Britain, the United States and people from Nazi-occupied countries, pledged that, when the war was over, Nazi war criminals would be tried.

The trials began at Nuremberg, Germany, on November 20, 1945, and covered 403 court sessions. More than 100,000 captured German documents were studied by attorneys preparing for the trials. The court record of the proceedings at Nuremberg fills 42 large volumes. When the trials were over, 19 men were found guilty. Of those, 12 were hanged. Three men, found not guilty of crimes against humanity* even though they had been part of the Nazi leadership, were set free.[49]

"Nuremberg began an international enclave that was a hot spot for all sorts of political intrigue by our Allies, particularly the Russians, as well as the Germans," Kiel says. "There were some Allied personnel who had collaborated with the Nazis who remained in Germany, many in Nuremberg, afraid to go back to their native countries, fearing reprisals.

"I remember in particular a Dutch girl who had been confidential secretary to the Gestapo commander in the area. She insisted that she had been forced to do the work, but under interrogation, she admitted that her parents had been members of the Dutch Nazi Party, even before the German invasion of the Netherlands. Obviously, she never would have been placed in her position of confidentiality if there had been any questions of her loyalty. We notified the Dutch liaison officers, who had her arrested, and she was returned to Holland to stand trial."

When Kiel got to Nuremberg, he found that the older section of the city, bombed heavily by the British during World War II, was completely leveled. He compares the work he did in counter-intelligence to having a job with the "army FBI." Although he technically had nothing to do with the war criminals themselves, Kiel was amazed by the devastation in Germany that he saw in his 13 months in the country. Eleven of those months were spent at Nuremberg.

"Germany was desolated," he says. "The Germans were on short rations. ... Of course, there was no German who knew what had been going on. All of a sudden there were no Nazis around. Just as they possibly kowtowed to the Nazi hierarchy, they certainly, to a great extent, kowtowed to the, shall I say, occupiers or conquerors. In these comments, I do not mean to excuse the Germans. The average German was guilty. Although there were some Germans who helped, hid, did what they could for anti-Nazi feet. As far as I could tell, they adapted to the Nazi regime wholeheartedly."

In fact, Kiel says, he believes little was known about Jewish resistance to Nazi persecution for many years because the only records of the Holocaust that had been examined were Nazi records.

"It was only later that we were able to dig up, for example, *The Diary of Anne Frank.* ... Articles that were buried in the ground around the camps in Auschwitz showed up 15, 20, 25 years later. *The Diary of the Warsaw Ghetto**, I think, it was 18 years before it was possible to go back and find it.

"And the Nazis, of course, were going to show the decadence and the lack of feeling. And there was a reason for many of these people, as you saw in films, being so-called like the 'lamb being led to the slaughter.' If the will is completely washed out of people, if they have no food and if they are starving, their brains are affected, their will is affected, and they are like sheep. It doesn't make any difference what people you are.

"As far as blaming the Germans, to a great extent, that's an easy thing to do. And, of course, the Germans did follow like sheep, and this is a great danger anywhere, where one step at a time, we don't realize it, where you get a dictatorship, where you get power. The Germans, always a militaristic people, fell into the hands of the Nazis because the European powers allowed the Nazis victory after victory, feeding the national pride of the average German who closed his eyes to what was going on about him, but could only remember two lines of the German national anthem, 'Deutschland, Deutschland uber alles; heute Deutschland, Morgen der velt. Germany, Germany over everything; Today Germany, tomorrow the world.'"

For years, Kiel has pondered who to hold responsible for the Holocaust. He lives in Greensboro and is a retired furniture sales representative. To him, the blood of 11 million is on the hands of several nations.

---

*NOTE: *"The Diary of the Warsaw Ghetto"* is a record of the events leading up to and during the Warsaw ghetto uprising, a time when thousands of Jews, jammed into a ghetto in Warsaw, Poland, revolted aginst their Nazi persecutors.

"I'd say the world in general," he says. "The guilt cannot be pinned on just a person, a people, an evil ideology. Because, as long as there is prejudice, and to say there is no holocaust going on today, in any form, would be ridiculous. The leading Nazis in the first trials were tried for war crimes and for crimes against humanity. In that respect, the Nuremberg trials were a failure, because certainly you don't have to look very far to see crimes against humanity going on all over the world today. The trials were supposed to prevent that, and they did not."

So blame for the Nazis' genocidal destruction of the Jews, Poles, Gypsies and others lands on several doorsteps.

"The anti-Semitism of the medieval church, Protestant as well as Catholic is well-documented. I don't have to say anything about it," Kiel says. "It continued, of course, through the ages. It still was and is being taught in many of the European schools. And many of the schools in Europe are church schools."

Also at fault are the treaties of World War I, he says, "where the reparations virtually put all of Germany in not only poverty, but below-level poverty. (The Germans) didn't even have enough to eat. And, so it was a simple matter for a demagogue like Hitler and the other people to not only play on their fears, but to give them pride.

"I condemn, along with the leaders of France and England the United States, which never formally joined the League of Nations. The fact that they allowed them to take (territory) step-by-step. When he (Hitler) marched into the Ruhr and the Rhineland and neither France or anybody said a word, well, you could just imagine a boost of pride in the Germans."

Also, at fault, Kiel says, are the men who led Great Britain and France during the 1930s. They were "so intent on having 'peace in our time,'" he says, that those leaders did almost nothing to halt Hitler's gradual claim to territory belonging to other nations across the European continent.

"If they had moved against him in 1936 when the German Army marched into the Rhineland and remained firm in negotiations with him, I am convinced that not only would there have been no war, but that his downfall was inevitable.

"In conclusion, this does *not* lessen the guilt of the German people. They still bear the primary guilt."

CHAPTER 13
ANTI-SEMITISM

Who paved the way for Adolf Hitler and his henchmen to whip an entire nation into a whirlwind of xenophobic fury against their own countrymen? Were the Nazis just following orders? Was the German populace largely ignorant? Or did it know about the persecution — and extermination — of Jews, Gypsies, Jehovah's Witnesses and others dubbed "undesirable" by the Third Reich? How well-planned was the Final Solution to exterminate the Jews? Could the free world, particularly the United States, have done anything to stop the Nazi Holocaust?

Moreover, how do we — 40 years later — explain the behavior of millions of administrators, bureaucrats, civil servants, physicians, railroad workers, engineers, teachers, clergy and others who did their jobs, all along turning their heads to the persecution and death perpetrated by the Third Reich? American and European movies and literature are cluttered with tales of World War II heroism: daring Resistance fighters, guilt-ridden Czechs and others who hid their Jewish countrymen, and compassionate Allied servicemen stunned by the plight of the Jews as the war ended. But before the war, few free nations would take Jews. Those that did kept their immigration quotas tight, rather than expanding them, a move that might have saved millions of lives.

Missing from the popular accounts of World War II are details about the actions of the people who *allowed* the Jews and others hated by the Third Reich to suffer. We can pinpoint many of the perpetrators of the injustice. Unpunished are the bystanders.

119

In the four decades since Hitler committed suicide and the Third Reich fell, the list of questions has lengthened, not shortened. Nuremberg answered only part of the chorus of accusations against the Nazis. The determined efforts of the Israeli government and Nazi hunters such as Simon Wiesenthal have brought to justice only some of the hatemongers left at large at the close of World War II. Many believe Austrian leader Kurt Waldheim is among those. Authorities now believe Josef Mengele, chief physician at the Auschwitz death camp in Poland, never was captured. Sought for arrest by West Germany since 1959, Mengele is thought to have drowned in 1979 in South America after living there in hiding under an assumed name. But some survivors, particularly the thousands of twins upon which the "Angel of Death" performed his notorious genetic experiments, refuse to believe Mengele is dead.

To the survivors of the Holocaust, the remaining questions are not the benediction to a closed chapter in history, but an invocation that pleads for the world never to forget the 11.5 million Jews and others who perished.

As a Southern Christian in grade school, I remember my favorite teachers noting the adage that "history repeats itself." As a college student, I recall that some Southern history professors believed that the South as a region would long be scarred by its refusal to grant full rights to blacks. In Sunday School, I was taught about "one great fellowship" of Christian love.

Yet when I first began writing this book, only Jewish people and a handful of friends and relatives seemed to understand why 40-year-old tales of concentration-camp death and brutality were important to me. The lessons I had learned as a child and a young adult seemed to apply to the horror of the Holocaust. And I seemed to have a natural responsibility to do something about preventing such sin from being perpetrated again. But many I talked to didn't see it the same way. Only survivors really seemed to know why I wanted so fiercely to tell their stories.

Werner Weinberg, a professor of Hebrew language and literature at Hebrew Union College-Jewish Institute of Religion in Cincinnati, Ohio, says most survivors tell their stories to keep another Holocaust from occurring.

"Whether one likes it or not (and I do not), the idea of doing all in one's power to prevent a recurrence (another cliche) is, in one form or another, the most frequently cited reason for survivors to tell their tale. I admit to having used it myself occasionally; to give my endeavor a respectable educational appearance, or to frighten my audience into participation," Weinberg writes.[50]

"But do I really believe that such an educational effort is effective? Can I conceive that my story, or even those of a few thousand people like me, could prevent another Holocaust?

"The answer has to be 'No', if certain conditions all came together again: (1) an economic and political situation as desperate as it was in Hitler's Germany; (2) the rise of a new evil genius with Hitler's demagogic powers; (3) virulent and all-pervading anti-Semitism; (4) repeated use of the 'Big Lie' with mastery; and (5) an entire nation's being stricken by megalomania and arrogance, the curse of pseudoscience, and by the deadly combination of sentimentality and cruelty. Then humankind could stumble into another Holocaust, no matter how convincingly the horrors of the last one are retold."[51]

Both historians and theologians have laid part of the blame for the Holocaust at the feet of the church. There were instances of Christians hiding Jews and other persecuted groups from the Nazis. During the war, there were Christian voices of dissent like Dietrich Bonhoeffer and Martin Niemoeller. And there were Christians who died much like their Jewish brothers and sisters. But the church, by and large, was silent as the Nazis gradually spread their anti-Semitic propaganda. Some believe the Holocaust was the culmination of 1,600 years of hatred of Jews.

"Christianity did not create the Holocaust; indeed Nazism was anti-Christian, but it made it possible. Without Christian anti-Semitism, the Holocaust would have been inconceivable,"[52] say Dennis Prager and Joseph Telushkin, authors of *Why the Jews?*, a book about anti-Semitism.

Prager and Telushkin detail centuries of church-fostered anti-Semitism that began with the editing of the New Testament and continued through the Protestant Reformation. Among the many instances they cite is a case in 1329 in Savoy. In that instance, "Christians claimed that the Jews compound out of the entrails of murdered Christian children a salve called aharance (haroseth), which they eat every Passover in place of a sacrifice; they prepare this food at least every sixth year because they believe they are saved thereby."[53] So simple was it for a sacred Jewish holiday and a simple food of bitter herbs to be misrepresented that few Christians, at the time, questioned the truth of the story. Six centuries later, the Nazis renewed the charge in a May 1, 1934, issue of the Nazi newspaper, *Der Sturmer.* That issue was devoted to Jewish ritual murder.

More recently, Jewish leaders have been deeply angered by the anti-Semitic tone of the script for the famous Passion Play, performed periodically in Oberammergau, a town in Bavaria, in Southwest Germany. Closer to home, Jews and Christians alike are disturbed by the resurgence of neo-Nazi organizations and the Ku Klux Klan in North Carolina and other states.

Leaders of both factions have been prosecuted and convicted of violent crimes in 1986 and 1987. Even before, the Anti-Defamation League of B'nai B'rith kept close tabs on their activities. In spite of their visibility, both groups are smaller than they once were, the ADL said in a special report, "Propaganda of the Deed: the Far Right's Desperate Revolution." That report details robberies, a synagogue bombing, shoot-outs with FBI agents and an assassination.

All were spearheaded, the report says, by an "underground network of armed racists and anti-Semites" committed to over-throwing the United States government.[54] In spite of the good track record of law enforcement agencies in running down and arresting the leaders of organizations involved in such criminal activities, their influence remains a dangerous one. They go by names such as "The Order," "Bruders Schweigen" (German for Silent Brotherhood) and "Aryan Nations."

Richard Butler founded the Aryan Nations organization in the early 1970s and moved it from Southern California to Hayden Lake, Idaho. "The organization is associated with Butler's 'Church of Jesus Christ Christian,' and he has tried to make use of this religious affiliation to avoid payment of federal, state and county taxes," the ADL report states. "The 'Church' adheres to the 'Identity' doctrine, an anti-Semitic concept which contends that white 'Aryans' are God's true chosen people and the Jews are instruments of Satan who should be eliminated."[55]

The ADL and other anti-Klan and anti-Nazi groups are disturbed by the emergence of computerized networks linking right-wing activists. Anyone with a home computer and modem (telephone hookup) can access the networks by dialing a telephone number. Most of the network's information is hate propaganda, but one network lists purported enemies of right-wing groups and includes a listing of the offices of the ADL.

"There are indications that the current wave of right-wing terrorism may not yet be over," the ADL report says. "Some Klan and neo-Nazi figures appear to have gone underground. There may also be other clandestine terrorist units, operating autonomously, that have not yet surfaced. Several heavily armed hate groups continue to engage in paramilitary training. A posture of alertness on the part of law enforcement agents as well as those who are potential targets of right-wing terrorist acts is therefore advisable."[56]

Far-right activists have not gained in political influence or power, the ADL says. Their revolution has failed and they remain a small, vocal minority.

"The challenge they pose is to law enforcement authorities, who need to watch them carefully for any unlawful behavior, and to the rest of society, especially the youth, which needs regularly to be reminded as to what history reveals can happen when bigotry triumphs."[57]

EPILOGUE

It was a Tuesday night. I got home from work, started dinner and began making phone calls.

The first number was busy. No one answered the second one. I almost gave up for the evening. But the pressure to make contact with the survivors and liberators made me keep trying.

Two more calls. Two more unanswered numbers.

I dialed the next number. A man answered the telephone. He did not know me. I explained what I was writing and why I wanted to talk to him. He was polite, but evasive, noncommittal. He had already been interviewed, he said.

For another book? I asked. No, by a television station, he said. He had also talked to newspaper reporters in the past. Couldn't I look up those clippings, talk to those other reporters?

Well, yes and no, I said. We want original material for this book, I said. And we're trying to set up a permanent historical file, a collection of oral histories, on survivors and liberators. So I would really like to hear his experiences firsthand.

I know, I know, he said.

I tried again.

The idea, I explained, was that the book could be used by high school and college students, by civic clubs, church and synagogue classes, by individuals studying the Holocaust. We wanted people to know why the Holocaust should not be forgotten.

Again, he said, I know, I know.

I kept talking.

He listened quietly, politely.

Finally, I ran out of reasons, explanations. I was quiet.

A pause. I waited for him to speak.

Look, he said, I know what you're trying to do, but I just don't want to talk about it anymore. I'm really not interested. Do you understand?

Yes, I said, I understand. But I did not. The conversation left me tense, irritable and confused. Why didn't this man want to talk to me?

Didn't he understand the long-term significance of what we were trying to do? The conversation left me dissatisfied, but I had other people to talk to, other stories to gather.

That was almost four years ago. When I remember my reaction to that quiet man's reservations about an interview, I laugh at my own naivete and regret my insensitivity. All the frustration, all the irritation I felt that night are gone. In their place is empathy. Sometimes, after an interview with either a survivor or a liberator, I also want to forget all that was said, all the horror, all the evil revealed in that person's story. Most of all, I wish I could wipe out all the pain that reliving that evil causes each person I have interviewed.

Like a snake inching along wet concrete, the horrors of the Holocaust have wormed their way into my consciousness. They've left a lingering feeling of the senselessness of prejudice, the idiocy of hate, the fragile reality of freedom and the evil always lurking behind the facade of modern civilization.

I think about the real people of the Holocaust every time I read a book, see a film or watch a television program even remotely connected to Nazi Germany or World War II. And, often, I can think of nothing to say, no way to explain why it happened.

So now I understand, maybe only a little, what the man who didn't want to talk to me was really trying to say through his simple refusal.

To publish one set of oral histories chronicling an unspeakable evil does nothing to dispel its continuing presence. It does not make it any easier to forget, any less painful to remember. It does not change the past, assuage the evils of the present or ensure that the future will be better.

Instead, it records, strives to document the horror we now know actually occurred. Like one man's silence, it is but a small part of a testimony that will never end. On trial in the court where the testimony is heard is all the apathy the human race sometimes shows in the face of injustice.

The 11.5 million who died because of the Nazis cannot testify. Only the survivors can testify. Only they can help us part the veil and see ourselves as we really could become if we stop fighting racial and religious prejudice, stop fostering interfaith understanding, stop protecting human rights around the world.

Whether the survivors alive today speak out or remain silent, theirs is a testimony that never ends. Because of them, the

APPENDIX I

THE SURVIVORS, CHILDREN OF SURVIVORS

GIZELLA ABRAMSON: Born Gizella Gross on August 22, 1928, in Poland. As a teenager worked for the Resistance. Emigrated to the United States in May 1946 to live with an aunt and uncle in New York. Moved to North Carolina when her husband, Paul Abramson, who was transferred with his company, IBM. Father, mother and younger brother killed in the Holocaust. Has two children, Michael and Holly Abramson. Abramson lives in Raleigh.

SUSAN CERNYAK-SPATZ: Born Suse Eckstein on July 27, 1922 in Vienna, Austria. Survivor of Auschwitz. Emigrated to the United States as the wife of an American serviceman in 1946. Moved to North Carolina in 1972. Now married to Hardy L. Spatz. Her mother died in the Holocaust. Her father survived. Has three children, Jacqueline, Todd and Wendy Fishman. Cernyak-Spatz lives in Charlotte.

WALTER FALK: Born June 5, 1927, in Karlsruhe, Germany. Left Germany in 1939 before the war started. Emigrated first to England, then to the United States to New York City in 1944. His father died before World War II began. Both his mother and his grandmother died in the Holocaust. Moved to North Carolina in 1960. Married to Ginger Falk. No children. Walter Falk lives in Greensboro.

FLORENCE GOEMAAT: Born Faga Sara Niedzwiedz on December 24, 1948 in Bergen-Belsen, Germany. (Bergen-Belsen, formerly a concentration camp, was a displaced persons camp after the war.) Daughter of Morris and Sally Niedzwiedz, both survivors. Emigrated to the United States in July 1950. Came under the auspices of the USA-United Jewish Appeal to Newark, N.J. Moved to Washington, D.C., in 1972. Moved to North Carolina in 1978. Moved to Warren, N.J., in 1986. Married to John F. Goemaat. Has three children. Florence Goemaat still lives in New Jersey.

DONALD HEKLER: Born Donald Leon Hekler on Sept. 21, 1947, in Asheville, N.C. Son of Ursula and Norman Hekler, both survivors. Donald Hekler lives in Annapolis, Md.

ERICA HEKLER: Born Erica Naomi Hekler on Oct. 13, 1959, in High Point, N.C. Daughter of Ursula and Norman Hekler, both survivors.

ANATOLY KIZHNERMAN: Born on December 7, 1937, in Zmerinka, U.S.S.R. Survivor of Jewish ghetto that was disputed territory during the war. Emigrated to the United States on July 10, 1980, to North Carolina on March 21, 1981. Married to Rachel Kizhnerman, also a survivor. Both of Anatoly Kizhnerman's parents survived the Holocaust. He has one son, Jerry Kizhnerman. Anatoly Kizhnerman lives in Greensboro.

KLARI KLETTER: Born on May 24, 1930, in Rosvegovo, Czechoslovakia. Survivor of Auschwitz. Emigrated to New York City in 1946 as wife of an American serviceman. Moved to North Carolina in 1974. Now separated from her second husband. Her mother survived the Holocaust. Her father did not. Has five children, Adrianne, Karen, Dana, Wendy and Robert. Kletter sold her home in Greensboro in August 1984. Since then, she has lived in New York City and Florida, returning to Greensboro occasionally to visit friends.

ESTHER MORDECHAI: Born Esther Politis on Dec. 25, 1929, in Jannina, Greece. Survivor of Auschwitz. Her first husband, Menahem Moshios, died in the Holocaust as did both her parents. Married Elias Mordechai. Emigrated to the United States on Oct. 4, 1951, through the United Jewish Appeal. Came directly to Greensboro, N.C. Has two children, Evelyn and Anny Mordechai. Esther Mordechai lives in Greensboro.

ELIAS MORDECHAI: Born Elias Nisim Mordechai on Oct. 10, 1910, in Jannina, Greece. Survivor of Auschwitz. Both of his parents died in the Holocaust as did his first wife, Sarah, and his daughter, Voula. Emigrated to the United States with his second wife, Esther, on Oct. 4, 1951. Has two children, Evelyn and Anny Mordechai. Elias Mordechai died in August 1987..

BRAMY RESNIK: Born Abraham Resnik on June 29, 1929, in Prague, Czechoslovakia. Survivor of Mogilev. Emigrated to the United States in June 1951. Moved to North Carolina in 1968. Both of his parents survived the Holocaust. Married to Rhea Ruth Schwartz Resnik. Has two children, Collette Beth and Howard Seth. Bramy Resnik lives in Greenville, N.C.

BURT ROMER: Born Berthold Roemer on Aug. 18, 1926, in Hennweiler, Germany. Survivor of Theresienstadt. Emigrated to the United States on January 25, 1948. Moved to North Carolina on Oct. 27, 1957. His mother died in the Holocaust. His father survived. Married to Alice C. Romer. Has one daughter, Helen. Burt Romer lives in Greensboro.

EVA WEINER: Born Chawa Sosna on May 25, 1916, in Rovno, Poland. Survived by hiding from the Nazis with her daughter, sister and niece. Emigrated to the United States in 1949, settling in Philadelphia, Pa. Moved to North Carolina in 1977. Married to Meyer Weiner. Has one daughter, Shelly Weiner. Eva Weiner lives in Greensboro.

ROCHELLE (SHELLY) WEINER: Born Rachel Weiner on Aug. 25, 1937, in Rovno, Poland. Survived by hiding with her mother, Eva. Emigrated to the United States in 1949 to Philadelphia after living in a displaced persons camp with her parents in West Germany. Moved to North Carolina in 1972. Married to Frank Weiner. Has three children, Donna, Debra and Julie. Shelly Weiner lives in Greensboro.

THE SERVICEMEN:

GLENN FARTHING: Born June 24, 1922, in Valle Crucis, N.C. Infantry officer during World War II in France and Germany, with the 7th Army. Among the troops at Dachau immediately after the camp was liberated. Farthing lives in Advance, N.C.

MORRIS KIEL: Born June 25, 1916, in New York City. Moved to North Carolina in 1947. At Nuremberg during the war crimes trials. Kiel lives in Greensboro.

CARLTON RAPER: Born Feb. 21, 1916, near Colfax, a small community in Guilford County, N.C. Raper entered the army in December 1942. He served in an engineer combat group. He was among the American troops at Dachau shortly after liberation. Raper lives in Pleasant Garden, N.C.

APPENDIX II

EXERCISES FOR STUDYING THE HOLOCAUST

One of the hardest parts of studying the Holocaust is developing real empathy for its victims. Survivors, even though they are alive, were as victimized by the Third Reich as the 11.5 million Jews, Gypsies, Christians and others who died or were put to death by the Nazis. The following exercises are designed to help us all learn to identify with victims of persecution and, perhaps, learn to live in such a way that tolerance and understanding, not hate and fear, rule our world.

I. **KNOWING WHAT IT FELT LIKE: ROLE PLAYING.**

> **MATERIALS:** Yellow construction paper, white paper, scissors, black pens, straight pins.

> **TIME:** Approximately 90 minutes.

Step 1: Divide the class or study group into three smaller groups. The first group should be twice times as large as the other two groups. (For example, in a class of 30, make the first group a group of 14. Put eight people in each of the other two groups.)

Step 2: Each group should choose a leader or spokesperson for the duration of the exercise. In the first group, that person becomes the head of the Nazi party. In the second group, that person is a rabbi. In the third group, that person is a political protestor.

Step 3: First Group: Each group member cuts out a white circle, four inches in diameter, then draws a swastika on the circle. The "badge" is then pinned to each group member's chest.

Second Group: Each group member cuts out a yellow circle, four inches in diameter, then draws a large "J" on the circle. The "badge" is then pinned to each group member's chest.

Third Group: Give this group yellow and white paper. Have each group member cut out a circle, four inches in diameter. This group is free to draw whatever it pleases on its circles. But each symbol must represent something. The group could choose "P's" to represent Polish for each member, or each group member could choose a different nationality. The only restriction is the group cannot be Jewish or Nazi.

Step 4: Group I now takes charge of the class. Its members sit at the front. Its leader gives an impromptu five-minute speech on any subject related to the Holocaust. The members of Group II (Jews) must sit at the rear, all members seated together. The members of Group III sit in between the other two groups. When Group I's leader completes the talk, members of Group I and Group III are invited to comment. Allow 15 minutes for discussion. Group II's members must be silent throughout the discussion.

Step 5: Separate the groups again. Allow them 15 minutes to discuss their thoughts, feelings and reactions to the exercise. Have the leader/spokesperson record the group's responses.

Step 6: Bring the groups together for reports from each. Allow 15 to 30 minutes for reports and general discussion.

II. WHAT WOULD YOU CHOOSE?

(This exercise can be done in small groups or individually. Allow extra time if the choice is a "group" decision.)

MATERIALS: Pens or pencils and paper

TIME: About 30 minutes for each scenario and choice.

Read the following scenarios to the group or class. Then have them individually or corporately choose how they would respond to each situation. It may be wise to list the choices on a blackboard or newsprint tablet.

SCENARIOS:

A. Imagine that you are the German commander of a concentration camp. A trainload of 300 prisoners arrives. As the prisoners get off the train, you must send half to the left, to work in slave labor conditions; the other half to the right, to die in the gas chambers. Which of the following responses would you choose? Select only one.
(1) Send the able-bodied to the left; the sick and old to the right.
(2) Send men to the left, women to the right.
(3) Neither. I'd let them all go.
Why did you choose the response you chose? If you plan to

allow all the prisoners to escape, how will you do that? What will YOU do once they're gone? How will you explain your actions to your superior officers?

B. Imagine that you are the Jewish leader of a council of prisoners charged with making certain decisions in a transit camp. The SS commander of the camp tells you that he must ship out 50 prisoners because the camp is overcrowded. He will not tell you where the prisoners are going, only that you must choose 10 women, 10 men and 30 children. Your mother, father, uncle and first cousin are in the camp. How do you keep their names off the list? How do you choose the others that must leave the camp, knowing that it is likely you will send them to their deaths? Why did you make the choices you made?

C. Imagine that you are a prisoner in a concentration camp. Your barracks is located near a barbed wire fence. You are standing outside the barracks. You look across the barbed wire and see a man pushing a wagon loaded with potatoes. If only you could get some of those for yourself and your friend. You decide to: (1) Watch the man walk on by. (2) Call to him and see if he'll give you some potatoes. (3) Go back inside the barracks. Why did you choose what you selected? How often do you think the Nazis' prisoners made similar choices? What are the consequences of your choice?

III. UNDERSTANDING THE AFTERMATH.

Read aloud the following situation to the class or group. Then have each person write down how he or she would act in response to such circumstances.

SCENARIO:

You live in New York City. Forty years ago you were liberated from a concentration camp. You and your younger brother survived. He lives in Israel. One sunny afternoon, your grandson comes to visit. He has been studying the Holocaust in school. His teacher tells him that a poor German economy was the major reason Adolf Hitler succeeded in building his Third Reich in Germany. You disagree. Why did the Holocaust happen? What do you tell your grandson?

SELECTED BIBLIOGRAPHY

BOOKS:

Abzug, Robert H. *Inside The Vicious Heart: Americans and the Liberation of Nazi Concentration Camps.* New York: Oxford University Press, 1985.

Altshuler, David. *Hitler's War Against the Jews,* New York, Behrman House, 1978.

Brenner, Reeve Robert. *The Faith and Doubt of Holocaust Survivors.* New York: The Free Press, A Division of Macmillan, 1980.

Epstein, Helen. *Children of the Holocaust, Conversations With Sons and Daughters of Survivors.* New York: Bantam Books, 1979.

Gilbert Martin. *The Macmillan Atlas of the Holocaust.* New York: Macmillan, 1982.

Auschwitz and the Allies. New York: Holt, Rinehart and Winston, 1981.

Kohner, Hanna; Kohner, Walter; and Kohner, Frederick. *Hanna and Walter.* New York, Popular Library, Warner Books, Inc., 1984.

Meltzer, Milton. *Never to Forget: The Jews of the Holocaust.* New York: Harper & Row, 1976.

Moskowitz, Sarah. *Love Despite Hate: Child Survivors of the Holocaust and their Adult Lives.* New York: Schocken Books, 1983.

Prager, Dennis and Telushkin, Joseph. *Why the Jews? The Reason for Anti-Semitism.* New York: Simon & Schuster, 1983.

Rossel, Seymour. *The Holocaust.* New York: Franklin Watts, 1981.

Selzer, Michael. *Deliverance Day, The Last Hours at Dachau.* Philadelphia and New York: J.B. Lippincott, 1978.

Wyman, David S. *The Abandonment of the Jews, America and The Holocaust, 1941-1945.* New York: Pantheon Books, 1984.

Yancey, Phillip. *Where is God When It Hurts.* Grand Rapids: Zondervan, 1977.

Zweigenhaft, Richard L. and Domhoff, G. William. *Jews in the Protestant Establishment. New York: Praeger Publishers, 1982.*

MAGAZINES:

Lehman, Helmut T. "Nazi Germany: Lessons for Today," *The Lutheran,* August 1985, pp. 17-20.

Marty, Martin E. "The Century and the Holocaust," *The Christian Century,* April 10, 1985, pp. 350-352.

Weinberg, Werner, "Survivor of the First Degree," *The Christian Century,* October 10, 1984, pp. 922-926.

NEWSPAPERS:

"American Nazis Linked to Murders, Robberies, Counterfeiting." *High Point Enterprise,* 6 January 1985, Sec. 1, pp. 1A, 7A.

"Breaking the Silence." *St. Petersburg Times, Religion.* 17 November, 1984, p. 9.

"Book charges U.S., Britain never intended to rescue European Jews." *St. Petersburg Times, Religion.,* 17 November 1984, pp. 8-9.

"Dachau." *Greensboro Daily News.* 20 December 1978, p. A-4.

"Files report trial of Nazi Criminal." *Greensboro News & Record.* 24 January 1985. Sec. 1, pp. A1, A10.

"Shelly Weiner Relates Personal Experiences of the Holocaust." *Federation News,* (Greensboro, N.C.) May 1985, p. 6-7.

REPORTS:

Computerized Networks of Hate. Anti-Defamation League of B'nai B'rith, New York, Spring, 1985

The KKK and the Neo-Nazis. Anti-Defamation League of B'nai B'rith, New York, Winter, 1985.

Propaganda of the Dead. Anti-Defamation League of B'nai B'rith, New York, June, 1985.

INTERVIEWS:
Survivors, Children of Survivors

Cernyak-Spatz, Susan; October 22, 1984, Charlotte, N.C., at her home.

Falk, Walter; August 26, 1984, Greensboro, N.C., at Temple Emanuel.

Friedlander, Saul; October 15, 1984, Greensboro, N.C., at *Greensboro News & Record* offices.

Goemaat, Florence; August 26, 1984, Greensboro, N.C., at Temple Emanuel.

Hekler, Donald; March 31, 1985, Greensboro, N.C., at his home.

Hekler, Erica; March 8, 1985, Atlanta, Ga., at her home.

Kizhnerman, Anatoly; August 12, 1984, Greensboro, N.C., at Temple Emanuel.

Kletter, Klari; August 9, 1984, Greensboro, N.C. at Temple Emanuel. (Also September 9, 1985, Greensboro, N.C., at the home of a friend.)

Mordechai, Esther; September 16, 1984, Greensboro, N.C., at her home.

Mordechai, Elias; September 22, 1984, Greensboro, N.C., at Temple Emanuel.

Romer, Burt; August 5, 1984, Greensboro, N.C., at Temple Emanuel. (Also April 21, 1985, Greensboro, N.C., at his home).

Resnik, Bramy; March 23, 1985, Greenville, N.C., at his home.

Weiner, Eva; September 20, 1984, Greensboro, N.C., at Temple Emanuel.

Weiner, Rochelle (Shelly); September 20, 1984, Greensboro, N.C., at Temple Emanuel.

THE SERVICEMEN:

Farthing, Glenn; October 14, 1984, Greensboro, N.C., at his home. (Also April 20, 1985, Greensboro, N.C., at his home).

Kiel, Morris; October 11, 1984, Greensboro, NC, at Temple Emanuel.

Raper, Carlton; August 26, 1984, Greensboro, N.C., at Temple Emanuel (Also April 17, 1985, Greensboro, N.C., at *Greensboro News & Record* offices).

FOOTNOTES

[1]Saul Friedlander, interview at the *Greensboro News & Record* offices, Greensboro, N.C., October 15, 1984.

[2]Seymour Rossel, *The Holocaust,* (New York: Franklin Watts, 1981), pp. 45-47.

[3]Burt Romer, interview at Temple Emanuel, Greensboro, N.C. August 5, 1984. (Also April 21, 1985, at his home, Greensboro, N.C.)

[4]Elias Mordechai, interview at Temple Emanuel, Greensboro, N.C., September 22, 1984

[5]Esther Mordechai, interview at her home, Greensboro, N.C., September 16, 1984.

[6]Martin Gilbert, *Auschwitz and the Allies.* (New York: Holt, Rinehart and Winston, 1981), p. 337.

[7]Susan Cernyak-Spatz, interview at her home, Charlotte, N.C., October 22, 1984.

[8]Rossel, *The Holocaust,* pp. 33-35.

[9]Ibid.

[10]Walter Falk, interview at Temple Emanuel, Greensboro, N.C., August 26, 1984

[11]Rochelle (Shelly) Weiner, interview at Temple Emanuel, Greensboro, N.C., September 20, 1984.

[12]"Shelly Weiner Relates Personal Experiences of the Holocaust," *Federation News,* (Greensboro, N.C.), May 1985, p. 7.

[13]Eva Weiner, interview at Temple Emanuel, Greensboro, N.C.,

[19]Rochelle (Shelly) Weiner, interview, September 20, 1984.

[20]Anatoly Kizhnerman, interview at Temple Emanuel, Greensboro, N.C., August 12, 1984.

[21]David Altshuler, *Hitler's War Against the Jews.* (New York: Behrman House, 1978), p. 115.

[22]Ibid.

[23]Ibid.

[24]Gizella Abramson, interview at her home, Raleigh, N.C., May 5, 1986.

[25]Martin Gilbert, *The Macmillan Atlas of the Holocaust.* (New York: Macmillan, 1982), p. 36.

[26]"Holocaust survivor hopes lessons of horror will linger," *The News and Observer,* (Raleigh, N.C.), 22 September 1986, p. C-1.

[27]Gizella Abramson, interview, May 5, 1986.

[28]"Holocaust," *News and Observer,* p. C-1.

[29]Gizella Abramson, interview, May 5, 1986.

[30]"Despite pain, survivor feels need to tell story of Holocaust," *News and Observer,* (Raleigh, N.C.), 22 September 1986, p. C-1.

[31]Gizella Abramson, interview, May 5, 1986.

[32]Bramy Resnik, interview at his home, Greenville, N.C., March 23, 1985.

[33]Esther Mordechai, interview, September 16, 1984.

[34]Milton Meltzer, *Never to Forget: the Jews of the Holocaust.* (New York: Harper & Row, 1976), p. 185.

[35]Bramy Resnik, interview, March 23, 1985.

[36]Donald Hekler, interview at his home, Greensboro, N.C., March 31, 1985.

[37]Erica Hekler, interview at her home, Atlanta, Ga., March 8 1985.

[38]Donald Hekler, interview, March 31, 1985.

[39]Erica Hekler, interview, March 8, 1985.

[40]Florence Goemaat, interview at Temple Emanuel, Greensboro, N.C., August 26, 1984.

[41]Carlton Raper, letter, October 10, 1986.

[42]Carlton Raper, interview at Temple Emanuel, Greensboro, N.C., August 26, 1984. (Also April 17, 1985, at *Greensboro News & Record* office, Greensboro, N.C.)

[43]"Dachau," Greensboro Daily News, 20 December 1978, p. A-4.

[44]Glenn Farthing, interview at his home, Greensboro, N.C., October 14, 1984. (Also April 20, 1985, at his home, Greensboro, N.C.)

[45]Eva Weiner, interview, September 20, 1984.

[46]Bramy Resnik, interview, March 23, 1985.

[47]Klari Kletter, interview at Temple Emanuel, Greensboro N.C., August 9, 1984. (Also September 9, 1985, at the home of a friend, Greensboro, N.C.).

[48]Morris Kiel, interview at Temple Emanuel, Greensboro, N.C., October 11, 1984.

[49]Rossel, *The Holocaust,* pp. 121-124.

[50]Werner Weinberg, "Survivor of the First Degree," *The Christian Century,* October 10, 1984. p. 925.

[51]Ibid.

[52]Dennis Prager and Joseph Telushkin, *Why the Jews? The Reason for Anti-Semitism.* (New York: Simon & Schuster, 1983), p. 104.

[53]Ibid., p. 100.

[54]*Propaganda of the Deed,* Anti-Defamation League of B'nai B'rith, New York, June 1985, p. 1.

[55]Ibid., p. 8.

[56]Ibid., pp. 10-11.

2-16

CPSIA information can be obtained
at www.ICGtesting.com
Printed in the USA
LVOW04s1603221116
514097LV00011B/1049/P